"The 'tightrope' is one of the most apt metaphors for parenting I've ever read about. If you fall off on either side of the tensions, you're in trouble—and worse yet, so are the kids! Russ has been a student of navigating relational challenges for many years now, and it's great to have a guide who's walked the rope before you."

John Ortberg, teaching pastor,
Menlo Park Presbyterian Church

"This is not the 'right' approach to parenting, but it may be the best. No cookie-cutter strategies for raising fairy tale families in this book. This is reality parenting—a balanced dose of straight talk and timely wisdom for confronting the fear and confusion every parent faces. One day your kids will thank you for reading this!"

Bill Donahue, executive director of small groups,
Willow Creek Association

"Finally, a book on parenting by a man! This lawyer dad has real wisdom for parents (especially parents of teens). Grab a copy for all the dads you know!"

Susan Alexander Yates, author, *31 Days of Prayer for My Teen*

"If you are a parent, please read this book. If you know parents, please urge them to read this book. Drawing on his experience as a lawyer, church leader, and experienced parent, Russ Robinson has written a unique parenting book. It is practical, realistic, innovative, engaging, biblical, story filled, and fun to read."

Gary Collins, distinguished professor of leadership and coaching,
Psychological Studies Institute

walking the
parenting
tightrope

RAISING KIDS WITHOUT
LOSING YOUR BALANCE

Russ Robinson

BakerBooks

Grand Rapids, Michigan

Published by Baker Books
a division of Baker Publishing Group
P.O. Box 6287, Grand Rapids, MI 49516-6287
www.bakerbooks.com

Printed in the United States of America

Library of Congress Cataloging-in-Publication Data
Robinson, Russ
    Walking the parenting tightrope : raising kids without losing your balance / Russ Robinson.
        p.   cm.
    Includes bibliographical references.
    ISBN 0-8010-6552-6 (pbk.)
    1. Parenting—Religious aspects—Christianity. I. Title
BV4529.R625 2005
248.8′45—dc22   2005012317

To Lynn, Phil, Mark, and Tim
The one thing we will always have is family.

Contents

Acknowledgments

Most acknowledgments end with a final word of thanks to an author's family. The topic demands I start there. This book never would have happened without a lifetime of contributions from Lynn, Phil, Mark, and Tim.

Lynn has gripped my hand tightly for twenty-eight years of marriage and eighteen years of parenting. Sometimes she has held my hand to keep her from falling off the tightrope, and plenty of times she has done it to keep me balanced. The ideas discussed in these pages are often as much hers as mine, especially the small group lessons she initially drafted. Without her putting her inquisitive mind to reading almost every book she could find on child rearing we would be far less engaged and intentional parents. Our daily habit of huddling for conversation and prayer at 7:00 a.m.—something she fostered—has kept us together like glue. Her reading, rereading, re-rereading of this project . . . priceless.

Phil has been the lifeblood of our little community from day one; you tolerated all the "first child" experiments with a resilience that will make you stand strong through a life God has his hand on. Mark has played the middle child with incredible grace, often the grease on the gears without which we would grind to a halt; you give us hope all will be OK. Our family would suffer a missing link without Tim; you have managed to learn well from your older brothers while becoming your own, remarkable young man.

My parents, Clyde and Jeane Robinson, made an indelible mark on me. Their parenting affects nearly every thought you will read. Credit the good stuff to them, the questionable ideas to me. They deserve at least that for enduring the ups and downs of raising me! And to Rhonda and Rita, my sisters, many thanks for your love, tolerance, and forgiveness of a fallible brother whose growth came occasionally at your expense.

I owe a huge debt to my ministry partner and friend, Bill Donahue. His fingerprints show up in the first and last chapters, and in some of the lessons in the leader's guide due to our last book, *Walking the Small Group Tightrope*. After writing three books together, we each decided to go solo for our next projects, but I was far less intimidated than I would have been without Bill cheering me on. Although you beat me to the finish line with your manuscript, Bill, I am glad we could commiserate.

Meadowbrook Church, our "home away from home" where I pastored in New Jersey for two years, deserves credit for being the guinea pigs for the ideas that became this book. You gave our family a memorably warm welcome, and you gave me amazingly attentive ears and valuable feedback—I am grateful beyond words.

Chad Allen and the team at Baker made everything work so well. Their initial excitement about the concept for the book, encouraging words along the way, and skillful contributions to all aspects of the final product made all the difference in the world.

Janice Yarosh played editor late in the game and put just the right touches on the manuscript. That your scribbles came back with frequent cheerleading inserts and a container filled with cookies to get me to the finish line made you the hero, once again.

Every time you spot a name, read a quote, or trace a footnote, you will see the rich well of child-rearing wisdom from which we got to drink as parents. Lynn and I are unspeakably grateful for the treasure trove to which this is humbly added.

Foreword

From Tense to Tension

As a psychologist and a parent of two young girls, I have a problem. I see their day-to-day behavior sometimes, and the psychologist in me shudders as I project into the future. When my three-year-old pushes a limit or blames her sister for her own behavior, I immediately see drug addiction, prison, failed careers, and eight marriages in her future. I want to crack down and say, "Don't you see how you are going to ruin your life with that kind of pattern? If you are going to succeed, you have to take responsibility for your actions!" Then I look at the jelly on her forehead and realize that I may be a little ahead of schedule. I calm down and enjoy the moment, realizing that this level of maturity is about right and I will never get the chance again to negotiate with someone who wears oatmeal as makeup.

At other times, I get pretty tickled at their ability to live in the moment forever, not even knowing that there are other issues at stake. I can get lost in the hilarity of their immaturity and regress with them to the point of forgetting that there are other people in the restaurant who might not think that what is going on is as funny as I do. I need to impose some structure before we get thrown out.

11

And therein are the big questions of parenting. When do you just "be" with your kids and enjoy *who* they are and *where* they are, and when do you require that they "do" more than comes naturally? How do you balance the two extremes?

When I say that this is the big question of parenting, I speak not as a parent. I speak as a psychologist with over twenty-five years of experience working with people carrying the burdens of their parents' poor parenting and also with parents who are in the process of parenting itself. A *huge* percentage of problems that people have is because of an imbalance of extremes.

Beginning in infancy, the arguments rage. One group practically wants you to starve and deprive babies with limits, schedules, and structure so that the little sinner does not get control of the house. The other extreme comes back and says to give in to their every whimper and let them take over the parents' bed until it turns into the family garage. Some say you had better have immediate obedience as they get a little older; others advise laying off so you won't hurt their precious self-esteem, whatever that is.

The problem gets to clinical proportions when parents camp out in one extreme or the other. As Solomon said, "It is good to grasp the one, and not let go of the other. The man who fears God will avoid all extremes. Wisdom makes one wise man more powerful than ten rulers in a city" (Eccles. 7:18–19).

To me, that is the great value of Russ's message to parents in this book. The answer to most every parenting problem is to realize that either answer you are contemplating is probably wrong. What is right is to be wise enough to utilize the good parts of both love *and* limits in a way that does not sacrifice either. Because if you don't exercise balance, your child may spend the rest of his or her life looking for the other end of the spectrum that you omitted. Too much discipline, and they might seek freedom in ways that could kill them. Too much freedom, and they might continue to be out of control until they find someone strong enough (like a judge or prison system) to finally contain them.

12

Russ has given us a great reminder that the right answer is one of balance. You may not agree with every solution he proposes in every circumstance. In fact, his message itself says you shouldn't, as it may not be the right balance in your situation. But what you should find agreement with is the *main* message: that bad parenting is always found in the extremes and that wisdom is in the balancing act for each day, the "tightrope" of tension.

May God bless you as you walk that tightrope and move from being "tense," to being in the wonderful "tension" of giving your children the mixture of all that God provides in the right amount for each and every day.

Henry Cloud, Ph.D.
Los Angeles

1

Welcome to the Parenting Tightrope

Some Problems Can't Be Solved

Having a family is like having a bowling alley installed in your head.[1]

Martin Mull

Our confusion started early. We were like most parents are with their first child: we wanted to get it all just right. So we consumed every book, tape, and seminar we could get our hands on. It's a good thing we did, because our first son, Philip, proved to be one of *those* children who chill the spine of every parent, *the strong-willed child*.

At one point we stopped calling him Phil and informally changed his name to Mary, Mary, Quite Contrary. It wasn't just that we'd say yes and he'd say no. We could say anything, ask anything, do anything, and Phil would find a way to say, respond, or act the opposite. From bathing to bedtimes, what to wear to what to eat, for any when, how, and why to do whatever, he maintained a different point of view. He was so good at it we often melted into laughter over his youthful creativity at contradicting everything.

I don't know where we read or heard it, but one expert categorically urged parents to confront such rebellion. In fact, the teaching prescribed the need to win the battle for a child's will in the first eighteen months, implying that if you didn't, the results would be catastrophic. Yikes! We were not laughing or employing nursery rhyme labels anymore. The clock was ticking, and eighteen months would be gone before we knew it! We girded ourselves for the battle to come.

In the next few weeks, every time Phil played his contrarian's card, we saw him and raised the stakes. That didn't faze him. After several rounds of an ever-increasing ante, we tried to play a trump card or two, such as life imprisonment on the time-out chair or no more ice cream ever, ever, ever again. Once in a while we won . . . until the next hour, when the subject changed. But our fight to break his extraordinarily strong will continued.

The pressure mounted as Phil closed in on eighteen months of age. Every passing day meant we were fast approaching long-term disaster. It was time for urgent action.

One day as my wife, Lynn, shopped at Target with our son, he started in. Lynn responded to each of his disobedient moves with correction, his unreasonable demands with an appropriate refusal, and his increasing volume with warnings of impending doom if he didn't stop it. Never one to back off from a fight, Phil kept at it until he decided it was time for a trump card of his own: the falling down, ranting, high-volume, embarrass-the-mom-enough-and-she'll-have-to-give-in temper tantrum.

That didn't deter Lynn. She had read the books. She knew just what to do. Except for one thing—the prescribed methods didn't work. Despite her best efforts to intercept bad behavior, this encounter was turning into the maternal death match:

a winner-take-all fight to the finish between a mother and her strong-willed son. She had to win, or who knows to what treacherous end Phil's life would lead him?

Nothing worked. Round after round she tried every trick in the parenting book, and it was getting worse, not better. Finally, in an act of sheer desperation, and if only to keep every shopper from gathering in Aisle 14 to see this battle royal, Lynn plopped on the floor, hugged Phil to her as tightly as she could, and joined him in a fit of sobbing born from months of trying so hard to get it "right" with her willful son. It was a defining moment.

Nothing changed with our quite contrary son and his unbending will. Phil's been consistent for all of his eighteen years. He has become a strong-willed man. Sometimes it serves him badly, because he refuses to learn anything other than in his own, frequently painful, way. But when he harnesses it for good, he has amazing passion, clear opinions, and novel solutions to problems.

The defining moment that day was for us. We realized how often the prescribed child-rearing answers don't work out in your real life the way they're described.

Did I Miss That Day in Class?

On more occasions than I can now count, Lynn and I have been left scratching our parenting heads. Most days we feel like you did in school when you realized you must have missed something, or you were gone the day other students learned the answer you need for the test in front of you. We keep wondering whether we blanked out in Parenting 101 for extended periods! Whenever our search for the best parenting practices led to a wide range of solutions with limited effectiveness, we became pretty convinced other moms and dads probably had the inside track on ideas we were missing.

17

Part of the craziness of parenting emerges when talking to other moms or dads. Take up any topic related to raising children, from spanking to schedules, dress codes to dating, education to eating, and every parent has a point of view. They are not usually loosely held thoughts, either. We parents embrace our ideas with deep conviction.

The higher your frustration level, the more fervently people will share their opinions about what you should do. Like you, we have been on the receiving end of such advice innumerable times. And, to our embarrassment, we've been on the giving end of glib judgments or mindless recommendations on how to be a "good" parent (apologies to all we've done this to!).

One of the early battles we fought with one of our kids was severe colic, which plagued our second son, Mark. From the minute we brought him home from the hospital, he was a nonstop bawling, coughing, snorting, spewing sound machine, a record setter for severity and duration when it came to colic.

It would never stop. No sooner would we fall asleep than he would crank up a colic fit. It wasn't only at night; some days Lynn would call my office by midafternoon begging me to come home just to give her a moment's relief. We would take turns holding him, walking him, even driving him around the block in hopes the motion would put him back to sleep. I would sit for hours with him saddled on one leg, my arm wrapped nearly Heimlich maneuver–style under his arms, bouncing him rhythmically in a manner that would release his endless supply of intestinal juices (a reader-friendly way to describe the mix of fumes and fluids). Friends, family, and the entire medical community were amazed at his capacity to disrupt a conversation, a party, a life with his unsolvable malady.

For the first few months after taking up residence in our home, he wore us out, and life as we knew it came to a screeching halt. There were no restaurant visits unless we wanted to endure the accusing stares all moms with a squalling baby know all too well. No babysitters to put up with the condition

18

(not more than once anyway). No end to the well-meaning counsel.

We, as his parents, just needed to do the "right" thing. At least that's what many told us. Everybody had a colic story to tell, which always ended with them, their sister, their neighbor, or (we concluded) their imaginary friend employing the magic solution to quick and painless treatment of colic of every kind. It was all so easy. For everyone but us. Mark just kept on crying, no matter what suggestions we tried.

And then when he was eight months old the colic up and left the building. Just like that, it was gone. We didn't spend a lot of time assessing which of the endless stunts we tried actually worked. We had our life back! No time to sit around and analyze what had just happened. It was time to rejoin society.

A couple of years after the colic abated, Mark started showing signs of severe allergies. An allergy specialist ran numerous tests to determine the exact nature of Mark's sensitivities. Far and away the number one problem: cat dander. Put him by a cat, and he would turn into a coughing, snorting, and soon-swollen sound machine, almost like a four-year-old with a case of colic.

Hmmm. Guess what. We had given away our two cats two years earlier, and his intractable case of colic had dissipated nearly overnight. Mark loved those cats. He would play with them whenever he could, and they loved nothing better than curling up with a warm, cuddly baby. Mark never had colic. He had cats!

The good news: now we have a glib response when we meet someone with a colicky baby. "It's probably just allergies," you'll hear us say. If you don't want to take our advice, fine. Be substandard parents. But colic is simple to deal with. At least it is now. As the old song says, "What's too painful to remember, we simply choose to forget."[2]

Why do we do this to each other? I suppose some of it is because people are eager to share what has helped them.

If you've cracked the code on helping a geeky junior high student to behave, adjust socially, and eat right; if you have the superhuman ability necessary to teach your child how to balance school, church, and family with TV, instant messaging, and current fashion demands while managing the latest crises with friends, zits, school project deadlines, or misplaced shoes, you probably deserve a medal along with the right to be heard.

But after many years of asking others how they handle a variety of family issues, I have to admit to some cynicism. Some advice sounded good but didn't work for me. Some advice came back to haunt its well-meaning source. One dad I know said no to a later curfew, but his son's surface-level compliance (described, of course, with great pride) was a mask for covert rebellion. The dad never knew, but my kids snitched when I later cited his decision to justify my refusal to let them stay out. One more good piece of advice gone bad. It's enough to make you crazy.

I've become convinced that the strength of passion over our ideas on how to parent is rooted less in certainty than in a variety of other emotions.

One of those other emotions is fear. We really don't know if we're getting it right, and it can take decades to tell if we did. So we cover our worry with reassuring talk, pretending to know we are doing well.

Another of those emotions is pride. Being a good mom or dad is an ego-enhancing experience. That is, when all goes well. When someone gets on a parenting roll, it's easy to let judgments about what everyone else is missing come fast and strong.

Joy and relief play into it as well. If you've wrestled long and hard trying to break through with one of your kids, whether it's potty training or finally putting down the video game controller long enough to get a paying job, most of us are so excited to tally a win that we talk about it to friends as if we have struck gold!

It's not just conversations with other parents that will make you crazy. It is the books, tapes, seminars, and infomercials too. Few publishing categories market their messages with greater fervor. I know, because I think we've bought most of what has been sold on raising kids.

Especially during those early toddler years, Lynn and I tried to read most anything we could find (to be honest, Lynn read most everything she could get her hands on and then gave me the benefit of her highlights). Although we gleaned some helpful hints along the way, we just didn't find that the day in and day out of being parents matched up with major segments of the early books we read.

The problem? Most of them left us with an impression, one I'm sure many authors didn't intend, that if we will simply do A, B, C, D, E, F, G, we will have great kids! It is portrayed, sometimes subtly and other times overtly, as a paint-by-the-numbers process. The truth, though, is this: we've seen parents who have done A–G, and some children didn't turn out so great. Then we've seen parents who not only didn't do A–G but have fumbled around and ended up with great kids. What's up with that? Why don't you automatically end up with bad kids if you make fundamental child-rearing mistakes?

1, 2, 3, Easy as Can Be . . . or Not

"Nothing has ever challenged and humbled me more than parenting." If these words were true for Pastor Bill Hybels, who created and leads a mega-congregation (Willow Creek Community Church), speaks to tens of thousands at a time, counsels presidents, flies real jets, races fast cars, sails treacherous seas, has written numerous books, and achieved the crowning feat of successfully raising two kids into early adulthood—if he put parenting above all life's challenges, I knew I was in for even more adventure in the coming days.

21

By then I had developed a nagging sense that what he said was true. Bill and I were in a small group at the time, about 1995 or so. Since we were all parents, we often discussed our common challenge: how to resolve the parenting conundrums we all faced. All of us felt like we were barely figuring most of it out.

My challenge by then focused on three boys, My Three Sons, as people familiar with the 1960s TV comedy would often label them. But Lynn and I rarely found our family situations as tidy as a half-hour sitcom. Maybe we lacked Fred MacMurray's wisdom or we needed Uncle Charlie in our midst.

Phil at age eight, Mark at six, and four-year-old Tim left us dazed and confused more than anything. Let me be clear: we didn't think they were going to end up maladjusted social pariahs. We simply had come to feel ill-suited to navigate the innumerable complexities of being a good mom and dad.

It wasn't for lack of preparation. Lynn and I both came from Christian homes that, though afflicted with some of the dysfunctions most families suffer from, were pretty healthy. Our parents had stayed together. They worked at their marriages. Sibling relationships were unbroken, and no major traumas interrupted our growing up. Our churches taught about biblically and emotionally workable family life, used the typical family-life films and curricula, and counseled parents on raising kids well. Like most people, we had even developed our own opinions about "good" parenting, so we could roundly criticize those who were messing up as parents.

Then we had children.

What Bill said was true for me. Parenting was vexing me more than anything I had done.

To this day, nothing has challenged me more. Take it on faith: I don't like to brag. But after leading hundreds of staff and thousands of volunteers at Willow Creek Church, overseeing ministries to families, students, and children, and managing two law firms—while litigating multimillion dollar cases, navigating nasty divorce and custody battles, and meeting families in their greatest grief and conflict over estates—raising kids easily outstrips all of it. I've endured the loss of our home to fire, written books, started businesses, and even pursued rock climbing, marathons, high-speed kart racing, and endurance motorcycle touring. But I agree with Bill. Nothing is more challenging . . . and humbling . . . than being a parent.

It's true, isn't it? Nothing produces more sleepless nights, perplexed thoughts, confused conclusions, blank stares, eruptive emotions . . . or overwhelming love, intense joy, recurring hope, resounding laughter, and profound sense of worth. We parents know there is nothing in life of greater value. But devoting ourselves to raising kids often drives us to the edge of insanity! As Phil hits adulthood, Mark is sixteen, and Tim is fourteen, we are ready to admit it.

When we turned from the books, good teaching, and friends' advice to face our real life challenges, something seemed to get lost. We wanted to raise Phil, Mark, and Tim to be godly, emotionally sound, socially adept, intelligent, functional men, but sometimes it didn't play out in real life quite like it was described on page seventy-three of the latest must-read, *How to Raise Perfect Kids*.[3]

An Introduction to Polarity Management

I was having lunch with my friend Wayne a few years ago. Wayne is one of the most voracious readers I know, one of those people who reads up to three or four books a week. I asked him what he had been reading lately.

He started talking about a business book called *Polarity Management* by Barry Johnson.[4] He was rereading it years after parking it on a bookshelf because he was facing some job issues he was having a hard time figuring out. Johnson's thinking had helped him earlier as an executive with the Levi

Strauss Company when he was seeking solutions to problems they were having.

This sounded intriguing, so I asked him for a simple example. On one hand, he said, a company like Levi Strauss has to figure out how to achieve high customer satisfaction by giving extraordinary value for the price they charge. Competing in the retail market for happy customers is tough, with shifting fads, steep discounts, and squeezed household budgets. On the other hand, a business needs to figure out how to make a reasonable profit, so they can grow the business. As those of you in business know, these days you have to exceed customer expectations, while making enough profit to pay generous bonuses, meet your credit obligations, and make shareholders giddy if you have them. Profit and customer service are two good things, but they are in tension with each other.

Wayne went on to describe how, as a business executive, he and his colleagues would work their fingers to the bone to figure out how to resolve this apparent contradiction. They felt like they had to have a solution, THE answer to do both.

In *Polarity Management,* Barry Johnson concludes there may be no answer; instead, he argues these two good things simply are in tension with each other, and there is no reconciling them. They are "polarities." All a business can do when they face polar opposite issues is to face reality: they have an unsolvable problem. What then? Rather than continue to expend energy, time, and money on a fruitless search for answers that don't exist, they can keep an eye on the tension between them. They have to manage the polarities, walking the tightrope strung between them without tilting too far to one side.

The conversation with Wayne produced one of those "aha" moments you sometimes have in life. I immediately started thinking about how this concept applied to many different areas.

Reflect on how many polarities exist in the church. We want to help spiritual seekers find the life Jesus offers them through our outreach and evangelism efforts. But what about providing care and discipleship, so the church meets believers' needs as well? Jesus says it so simply: "Therefore go and make disciples of all nations, baptizing them in the name of the Father and of the Son and of the Holy Spirit, and teaching them to obey everything I have commanded you" (Matt. 28:19–20). Four words—"go and make disciples"—create a set of polarities. "Go" means we reach out. "Make disciples" means we focus in. That little word—and—between "go" and "make disciples" is the tightrope churches have been falling off for almost 2,000 years. When do we shift resources away from reaching the unconvinced to edifying already somewhat mature Christians? Will we put the next dollar in the offering plate toward evangelism or discipleship, the Missions or the Christian Education department? Some churches conclude they must ignore one polarity for the sake of the other, concluding you can only be an evangelistic church or a disciple-making one. How do you keep both aims in play when they push against each other?

What do you do with the inherent tension created when two good things stand in tension with each other? If you apply polarity management theory, another response suddenly becomes available. You can say the previously unthinkable: "There is no solution to that problem."

I felt that way with my work at the time. I had stepped back from practicing law to take on leadership of the small group ministry at Willow Creek. No small challenge. I was charged with solving all the problems associated with connecting 20,000 people in community, while helping every one of our 4,000 small group leaders be effective shepherds. Our team, good as it was, had wrestled some problems within what felt like an inch of our lives. My discussion with Wayne triggered lots of thinking about how polarity management applies to small group ministry.[5]

There are many other examples outside business and the church. When something feels complex, you may be facing a set of polarities. Recognizing this won't take away the tension, just make it more bearable. Facing reality—that two good things have to get done—releases energy because you can constructively deal with both.

Polarity Parenting?

Not long after talking to Wayne, another lightbulb turned on for me. If the principles of polarity management applied to the little community of a small group, maybe they applied to the little community of a family, and the relationships between parents and their children. What if the problems Lynn and I kept running into couldn't be solved? Maybe there were some "polarities" in raising kids, good things that couldn't necessarily be reconciled.

For example, parents have two main jobs. (Actually, therapists agree that parents have 5,493,671,297,470,822 jobs to do. I am focusing on just two to make a point.)

One job is to create a nurturing environment that draws children into a safe, healthy family that sticks together through thick and thin. But parents also have to develop their children so they can leave the nest and enter the world's stark realities. The objective is to get this done by a reasonable age. (For parents, that's eighteen; for kids it's twenty-seven.) These two worthy goals—forming a close-knit family and developing competent, independent young adults—appear to contradict each other. If you're a parent, you know the tension you live with, especially as they age, to both embrace and release—to hold two good things in tension with one another.

The examples never end. The more you understand the principle and observe the world around you, the more often you will spot necessary polarities. Not every hard-to-solve problem can be stated in terms of polarity. Sometimes a challenge demands more focused attention, further experimentation, and increased creativity. But often, when a problem

26

proves intractable or extensive work results in failure, we may be missing the obvious.

The principles of polarity management suggest that in every area of life we must learn to manage the tension between two good things instead of trying to choose one thing over another. Business leaders strive to make a profit *and* please customers. Churches must evangelize *and* disciple. Good parents make every effort to build close, interdependent relationships with their kids *and* prepare them to live independently when they are grown. In these situations, choosing one thing over another is not an option—we must do both.

Managing tension keeps things in balance. Ask a tightrope walker. Properly stretch a nice taut rope between two good places—the start and the finish—and you get an exciting act. Loosen the rope at either end, and the task becomes impossible. Tension produces good results, and an informed and capable walker learns to manage it to his or her advantage. Often life works the same way. Not only is it a circus sometimes; you get to play the tightrope walker!

Keeping the Tension Right

Parenting is not, has never been, and never will be a paint-by-the-numbers deal. There's nothing wrong with a paint-by-numbers kit; it is a nice way to simplify the complexities of creating a masterpiece. Painting by the numbers will organize a color palette, but it will never rise to the level of being true art. Parenting is more about art than coloring.

Many of us can practice the art of raising children in a more masterful way by looking at it through the lenses of polarity management. Although I have considerably simplified the concepts of polarity management, the essence of the ideas, when applied to parenting, suddenly resolves much of the tension we feel as we strive to be the best moms and dads we can.

27

You will find that this book includes some parenting basics. Rearing children effectively is like any field or discipline, whether art, music, athletics, or carpentry. You have to know some fundamentals to be good at it. Understanding the "A through G" of parenting—and then some—matters. But there is no automatic formula for success any more than knowing how a socket set works makes me ready to build a NASCAR racer. Every parent needs to know some basics on child development, authority, education, spiritual direction, money management, and navigating the teenage years. Nothing you'll read in this book is contrary to the fundamentals of good parenting.

But as important as those things are, they cannot displace an underlying truth: effectively growing up kids is no dot-to-dot process where, if you draw straight lines in the right sequence, you'll get a beautiful picture. All that gets you is the false security of having matched up to someone else's formula for coloring book-level artistry. That is not parenting, though.

Parenting requires artistic achievement at a higher level, that of an acrobat who needs balance, daring, and ability to stay cool while many watch. It is the art of tightrope walking, managing dynamic tensions that constantly exist in the context of every family.

Every parent, and even every child, must come to grips with this reality. If you do, it may just be the most freeing experience you will find in the process of parenting well. Master the fundamentals whenever you can. But be prepared to manage the real tensions and challenges of everyday family life. Very often you'll find there are no right answers to some problems—just several good values and practices that you're trying to balance. Like walking a tightrope, parenting is exhilarating and dynamic.

Over a long time, I observed these principles at work in my own family. I also reflected on my growing-up years and looked over the fence at the innumerable "laboratories" I've watched parents run in their homes. As I began evaluating the experiences and learning of many parents, including my wife (who remains one of the best parents I know), I was able to identify at least six tensions every parent faces. The list is not intended to be exhaustive, and you will probably discover more along the way. But these six sets of competing needs capture much of what parents wrestle with as they try to raise children into functional adults, even into grown-ups who will change the world.

When you feel frustrated by your latest parenting dilemma, perhaps what you read here will relieve your stress. There may be no answer available. You may be wrestling one of those "unsolvable problems"—squarely planted between two good things, but your job is not to find an answer. Instead, you have no choice but to manage the dynamic tension between them.

Walking the Parenting Tightrope will address these six tensions in the form of a challenge continuum picturing the "pull" you feel when standing in the middle of seemingly opposed polarities:

The training challenge:
Limits ———————————————— Freedom

The discipline challenge:
Punishment ———————————— Nurture

The spiritual challenge:
Tradition ————————————— Choice

The adolescent challenge:
Tender Love ——————————— Tough Love

The financial challenge:
Support ———————————— Self-Sufficiency

The interdependence challenge:
Attachment ——————————— Autonomy

29

Parents who focus unduly on either end of the continuum will lose the balance great child-rearing demands. In fact, many proposed solutions we moms and dads try won't work because they will knock us, and our kids, off kilter. We can't choose limits to the exclusion of freedom, punishment without nurture, traditions over ultimate freedom to choose. It will take both family and institutional input for effective education, safety, and consequences for behavior to be shaped successfully. And it will take a tricky combination of unconditional and tough love to navigate adolescence. Give support without advancing self-sufficiency, or tip too far to the bonding side of relationship, and your children will be permanent residents in your home! Dynamic, effective maturation of your children means you must embrace the opposing ends of each continuum and walk the tightrope between them. Which competing objective is right? Both. What's the right answer? Yes.

Every family faces these six tensions. Each one represents the aspirations we have as parents: to have families that teach children how to live well within limits, accept authority, mature spiritually, and grow intellectually. Every mom or dad I know wants to see their kids learn how to take appropriate risks, become loving in all their relationships, be well prepared for vocational success, and eventually make it to the stage where they have adult friendships with their own children. How do you get all that? By embracing the tension.

After we've examined each of these six issues together, I think you will come to a realization. Whether you look at yesterday, today, or the years ahead, if you feel like parenting is like walking a fear-inducing, thrill-giving, hang-on-for-dear-life high wire act, it means you get it.

Some of the best moms and dads I know live on the tightrope. All six sets of tensions, individually or in some seemingly tangled mess, will keep you moving—you'll be feeling calm and under control only to be knocked off balance the next moment. But if you embrace child-rearing reality, you will stay energetically engaged in the adventure even when it feels like a circus gone awry. It won't make it easy. It might help give you a sense of sanity, though.

A Road Map for Using This Book

I always get out a map before a trip, just to get oriented for the journey. Our trek toward understanding how to walk the parenting tightrope will take us through eight chapters: this introduction, one chapter for each of the six challenges, and a conclusion. Each chapter will take us on a side trip of its own, where we will define each parenting challenge, describe some of what happens when we tilt too far to one end of the continuum, and then suggest some principles, tools, and ideas to keep us upright and steady when imbalance threatens our effectiveness. The conclusion will lead you to a leader's guide with eight lessons, one for each chapter, which you, your spouse, or a small group or class can use to process further biblical material, assessments, and other exercises. This guide can help small group leaders or class teachers navigate their groups through these ideas.

I hope the opportunity to look at raising kids from this new perspective will be, for you, a little like getting on an airplane is for me. Sometimes, when navigating life on the ground (even with a good map) becomes confusing, getting thousands of feet above it enables me to see things differently. Moms or dads who have embraced the idea that their toughest quandaries with children are more polarities to be managed than problems to be solved will see parenting in fresh ways. They will not only find freedom from well-motivated but unworkable, even naive answers, they will more often enjoy the ebbs and flows of authentic family life.

Some parents have told me how relieved they feel that someone finally told the truth about how raising children really works. Since I've had a varied vocational path, my opportunities to engage parents have included pastoral counseling, legal consultations over marriage breakdown or estate planning, ministry planning meetings, sermon or classroom teaching, and small group discussions. One thread is common: a mom or dad carries the weight of failure from trying to follow a system or connect supposed orderly dots. After some conversation, counsel, and learning, they realize that many of their perceived mistakes have simply been a reflection of reality in the life of a family. Instead of being overwhelmed by failure, they can diagnose the unsolvable problem and embrace a "tightrope mind-set." Likewise, you will see how viewing yourself as managing a tension will free you to navigate your way into increased effectiveness, and escape previously one-dimensional thinking you may find you've grown into.

It does not stop with parents, though. I like it when kids join their parents in the tightrope way of thinking. At a certain age or stage of development, children can digest this idea, and it will help them in the equally difficult job of growing up. When everyone in a family can identify the tightropes they are walking together, not only will they have common language to help them communicate, but they will have a way to increase engagement just when kids are detaching prematurely from family issues they want to ignore. It may even help you navigate some of the undue controversy that afflicts adolescent relationships. And it will set your children up to start their own families firmly rooted in reality.

One further word to churches: if a pastor, small group leader, or Sunday school teacher guides members through this study, it should help everyone in your church better understand how to encourage parents and guide them in staying on the tightrope. While each church needs to endow parents with some basic training, parents often need more. It's good to build baseline skills, but helping moms and dads understand the tightrope they're walking could help too. Not only will it give you a reality check on how you discuss family dynamics, it will also enable you to distinguish real problems from normal tensions in family life. It should also help parents reduce some of their adverse judgments of parents who aren't "doing it right." And anything you can do to help all families cheer each other on when they tackle the challenges of parenting will build the sense of community your church experiences.

Final Instructions before Tightrope Walking

The parenting challenge takes on many shapes, often unique to each family. Many of you are single parents or are dealing with the complications of blending a family. Special needs in some children—learning disabilities, physical disabilities, and emotional development issues to name just a few—add to the intricacy of an already tough task. Some of you parent an intact family with your spouse, but even you know the baggage just one husband and wife can import to their parenting style. Even simple differences in how women and men view a child's progress complicate the numerous decisions that have to be made to treat specific situations.

So how does this approach apply to every family? While I can't help but write from a guy's perspective, rooted in two families (mine, and my parents') with two marriages that survived, often against odds few knew about, I can vouch that the principles make sense. Having been regularly humbled, though, I encourage you to read with a mind as open as mine continues to be, but with a framework for interpreting what comes our way as parents.

First, whatever idea is presented, apply it with wisdom to your situation. Whenever parents decide a course of action, they must deal with their own marital dynamics (a tightrope of its own), family setting, and the personalities and behaviors unique to their own children. You may find the exercises in the leader's guide will help, because they will move you from theory to reality. Do the "homework" to help you determine what really will work in your situation. Whatever you do, don't lose the point of this book by translating it into a hard and fast set of rules!

Second, focus as much on how you think as what you think. Along the way, you will probably pick up some helpful tips you will want to put in play with your kids. You can evaluate what you think about how a particular idea will work in your family. But even more important than the overarching principle represented by each set of tensions is the mental process you will begin to create for yourself. How you think about your parenting challenges matters even more than what you do about them. Why? Because what you do may not work! Or it may work wonderfully with one child but not another. That is the nature of this tightrope. To stay on it, you will have to live with the tension rather than hope for magical resolution to what is certain to keep stretching you.

Third, not only will this expand your understanding of family dynamics—including why they're so often messy—but some of these ideas will have corollary principles for building community within the church. God uses the family as a metaphor for church life, so pay attention not only to the main point of family lessons for yourself, but for the church as family too.

We are all on a lifelong journey through these six challenges. If you're like me, you're hoping Proverbs 17:6 comes true in your life: "Children's children are a crown to the aged, and parents are the pride of their children." Some picture, huh? I think we all want that kind of crowning achievement.

By grappling with these tensions as positive, opposing forces, you can guide your children, and maybe your children's children, more skillfully. And perhaps your family will arrive at the point where it gratefully senses the reward for parenting done well. Getting there will require walking a tightrope.

Get ready for the adventure.

2

What Part of "No" Don't You Understand?

The Training Challenge

When you are little your life is up, the future is up, everything you want is up: wait up, hold up, shut up; mom, I'll clean up, let me stay up. Parents, of course, are just the opposite. Everything is down. Just calm down, slow down, come down here, sit down, put that down.[1]

Jerry Seinfeld

They met every two or three weeks, if only to have a few moments of conversation with adults. These seven mothers found each other through their church when they heard about some "Moms' Play Groups." The idea of enjoying some recreation with other mothers sounded good to them until they found out it was their infants and toddlers who were to do the playing. That was still okay; meeting together each week meant an hour or two (which is as long as the kids would last, really) of making some new friends.

The church provided them with some other moms too, who would help them deal with all the bewilderment of being initiated into the rite of motherhood. Eventually they realized this was a place where they could unload their frustrations in the company of others who were equally uncertain about what they had gotten themselves into, but it took a while.

Conversations in the early days started in harmless territory. What brand of disposable diapers is best? Who is your pediatrician again? Why don't our husbands help more? All these topics were not too dangerous, with pretty much any answer being acceptable. As the women spent more time together, they moved into riskier territory. Why did you stop nursing so early? What time do you put them to bed? Aren't you worried about feeding them that; it will ruin their teeth? When these moms started to put real opinions on the table, an increasing number of meetings ended with uncomfortable agreement to disagree about motherhood done right.

Eventually, though, every mother in the circle found out how clueless they all felt. It took only a few months for every child to melt down at some point during the play group meetings. Taking turns being humiliated by an insurrection of two-year-olds had a way of forcing everyone to be honest. Soon, everything got to be conversational fair game, since most times every mom was far less than certain on the best answer to the latest maternal riddle. Even with barely speaking toddlers, aggravation was uniform.

Taking It to the Limits

Much of the aggravation focused on every mom's unending battle over one simple word they were required to say about a million times each day: no. They would say it, say it again, say it a million times every day.

36

For a few years, no is the most dominant word in parental vocabulary. If only it would work! Of course, if it did work, raising kids would be a stroll in the park rather than a walk on a tightrope.

You hear it from toddlers as soon as they begin talking. You tell a two-year-old what to do, and what is one of their first vocabulary words? No! The same two-letter word we use as parents is twisted into a tool to defy limits. Sassing tots say no with annoying mimicry. And by the time they are six or eight they add vocal energy to the word: no! In middle school you start to get the "my parent is an idiot" look along with the no. In high school the no comes complete with commentary on how you are ruining your child's life.

Putting limits on behavior starts early in the life of every human being. Look at Adam and Eve. Moments after God conceives of a man and woman, he gives them limits. "Eat fruit from any tree," God says, "except this one. The fruit from this tree is out of bounds. The word on this one: No."[2]

God has his reasons for the limits he imposes. But even for his still sinless children, no was just the beginning of negotiations. Their free will meant choice. Adam and Eve blow through the stop sign at the first opportunity, best we can tell. And then they rush into a cover-up, complete with fig leaves and a nonstop flow of excuses. All of us have been having a tough time with limits ever since.

Limits on children come in all shapes at all stages:

Age 2: As long as you're in diapers, you can't . . .
Age 4: Until you start school, you can't . . .
Age 6: Even though you've started school, you can't . . .
Age 8: Until you get your grades up, you can't . . .
Age 10: Although your grades are good, you can't . . .
Age 12: As long as you behave that way, you can't . . .
Age 14: Until you learn to drive, you can't . . .
Age 16: Even if you have your license, you can't . . .
Age 18: As long as you're under this roof, you can't . . .

37

It's enough to make kids nuts. We as parents would be wise to recognize our own disregard for limits we don't like, whether we race past speed limits or procrastinate over time limits. The truth is that our kids watch us and often learn from us clever techniques for dodging as many no's as they can.

One of the most common ways they try to do this is by asking why? or why not? What they really want to know is this: when do the limits end or change? And that makes parents nuts too. So they respond with a very articulate, well-reasoned answer: "Because I said so." What parents mean when they say this is, "I am confused right now. I don't know when to give you freedom and how much of it to give you."

Freedom Is Never Free

"Why can't I stay out until midnight?" The first time that question gets asked is at about, oh, four years old, and it will be asked scads more times before a child leaves home. Has any parent figured out how to deal with that one? We haven't. Or at least we hadn't until John and Nancy Ortberg came up with a novel approach to the curfew debate with their oldest daughter, Laura.

Like us and many other adults, John and Nancy go to bed at a reasonable hour so they can get an early start on the next day. An adolescent clock like Laura's has different gears. Teenagers exchange early starts for late-night socializing, so they hit the doorstep at the last second possible, usually by the skin of their teeth. We all did it, but those memories get erased in the maternity ward. It will happen to Laura someday, but long after curfew controversies have cost her parents many pounds of parenting flesh.

John and Nancy stared at a future of fighting Laura over when to be home and told her to come up with a solution that would allow them to go to bed while enabling her to stay out later. Laura came up with a clever one: put an alarm clock set for midnight right outside their bedroom door. When she arrived home, she would shut off the alarm. If she was late, the alarm would go off, and it would cost her an earlier curfew for a while, in addition to an irritable set of parents. Laura got a little more freedom, but she had to walk the tightrope between that freedom and the limits her parents rightly imposed.

A child pushes for freedom at every turn. Any problem with that? No. It is a good and right thing. Each child is an individual who has his or her own ideas about how life should be lived.

When most parents think about the child-rearing job, they idealize it as a process of imparting to their kids a set of guiding principles for living life well, of endowing a child with their wisdom, partly passed on from their parents, and partly from their own life lessons. They want their kids to reflect their standards, what they think is important. If everything works according to plan, their children will be known for being from the "X" family by the way they conduct themselves and live out the family's ideals. On most issues, the parent would like the child to behave as the parent would in comparable circumstances. Getting to that outcome will require putting limits in place.

Learning to live with limits *and* freedom is a healthy part of the training process. We all know adults who didn't learn how to live in a world where the limits/freedom balancing act is a part of life. It usually means disaster.

Freedom is, in some ways, a goal we move toward. As Paul writes, "It is for freedom that Christ has set us free."[3] Staying enslaved to undue restrictions for your whole life means bondage. It does not mean we live with no limits, though. Instead, God envisions that his children will choose to be guided by an ever-maturing internal compass that reflects his way of thinking about every issue we confront. The Bible talks about it as eventually being "free indeed,"[4] reflecting "the mind of Christ"[5] due to my ability to "keep in step with the Spirit."[6] And yet, freedom isn't absolute. Understood and

39

exercised rightly, freedom means I choose limits for myself, knowing it can never be a license to sin,[7] or to offend those I should be on the lookout for.[8] It's a tightrope.

Ideally, every child walks a similar path toward increasing freedom, balanced by well-selected limits they choose. The external influence of parents must become the internal compass guiding them through life: they will have "the mind of mom" or "the mind of dad" (you hope they too exhibit the mind of Christ; we'll get to that on the spiritual challenge tightrope). They will walk through life guided by the spirit of limits once enforced by their parents.

Reins and chains have a limited shelf life. Pull on them too long or too hard, and a child's compass will go awry. Do without them, though, and a child will get lost quickly. Undue limits or overdue freedom can mean parenting breakdown.

Whenever you feel befuddled in trying to find the "right" answer on when you should loosen limits or pull back on the reins of one of your kid's freedoms, you are living in parenting reality. The tension between limits and freedom is a permanent fixture in the parenting picture, at least until they reach what the law prescribes as "the age of emancipation."

Take Them Chains Off of Me

But you can't wait until the age of emancipation to give a child freedom. Kids have to be given an increasing measure of freedom every day. They move from a crib where they live behind bars, to a "big bed" that lets them roam an entire bedroom. Once a child learns to stay in the yard, you can open the gate in the fence. They learn to look both ways when crossing the street and they can roam a neighborhood. Kids who know how to tell time and follow directions get to ride their bike to a friend's house.

When do you loosen restrictions? Sometimes the steps toward increased freedom are driven by the government: when most kids turn sixteen, they get their driver's license (although some states have delayed it until age seventeen). A driver's license is hardly about driving; it's about finding a kind of freedom real adults enjoy. But even when a clear age is defined there is still plenty of tension. Ask any parent of a new driver.

Usually, though, parents don't get the benefit of such clear timing. We have to decide when to retreat from the limits we have imposed, and how far to move toward freedom.

The process starts early. When our boys were small, we would often visit a local mall. Like most parents, we put them in strollers even after they could walk, belting them in simply to keep them in sight. They were not ready to be freed from that restriction and be cut loose in a large, potentially dangerous environment.

And yet there came a point when we had to set them free. Ten-year-olds won't fit in strollers! Of course, once out of the stroller, they had many more choices.

They chose to stay close most of the time. Once in a while they would get too far ahead. Or in Mark's case, his tendency to engross himself in any item of immediate interest would leave us looking around for a child oblivious to even having parents. (Lynn got paged to retrieve him twice on one brief trip to a grocery store—Twinkies got him the first time, seasonal toys the second.)

Going from belting them down to running loose was too large a leap to freedom, so we found a helpful solution in one of those baby accessory catalogues. We used a device with Velcro straps on each end, one for mom or dad's wrist and one for Phil, Mark, or Tim's wrist, and a retractable cord like you see on phones between them. The elasticity of the cord allowed them measured freedom. Wrist straps limited them just enough for our comfort.

We saw ourselves as progressive, creative parents. Many mall-walkers stared mercilessly at us for being parents who would, and I quote, "leash their sons like dogs." Despite fears of being reported for abuse, we ignored them. We had to make a choice between squirming, loud, or tantrum-throwing little boys who wanted out of a stroller, and keeping track of three unrestricted, energetic, periodically barbaric little boys. Picking either option would have drawn a different set of accusing glares. And regardless of the looks, we needed some middle ground to train our boys how they must behave in places like malls, parks, and other public places. Call it what you will, but the "leash" helped us move our kids through measured steps toward increased freedom.

Tolerating the stares of strangers is good preparation for later parenting challenges: as children get older, you get *their* glares. Regardless of what you decide about limits, your kids will meet you with the sneering retort, "You're so strict," followed by a recitation of the liberal and gracious policies of every other parent who walks planet earth. Occasionally you will hold your ground, other times you'll give in.

The space you give will be the proving ground for their readiness for more freedom, where you'll find out whether the move too far in the freedom direction will lead to good or to bad choices. If you learn your son or daughter was not quite ready for that much liberation, pulling back on the reins then is all the harder. So the next time you decide leaving limits in place is the wiser choice, only to find out several other parents were less strict than you months before. You're left wondering what the right answer is.

You're not crazy! Tension exists between imposing what matters to you as a mom or dad (limits) and a child wanting to make choices about how his or her life should be lived (freedom). What is the right answer? Yes. Should we guide children according to and inject our family values into them, and expect some level of compliance? Yes. Should we expect they will have opinions and make choices as they navigate life? Yes. Yes to both ends of the continuum.

It is *the training challenge*, and it looks like this:

Limits ——————————————————— Freedom

When it comes to the training challenge, what do you do with limits and freedom? Both. The right answer? A tension-filled *and*. It requires a process of training.

Walking the Training Tightrope

The Bible describes it this way in Proverbs 22:6: "Train a child in the way he should go, and when he is old he will not turn from it." Through parenting history, some have read those words as a promise, like if they paint by the numbers, God pledges a guaranteed outcome. If their child turns from what they were taught, they feel anger at God. When they loosen the rope only to watch one of their kids trip over it into bad choices, they feel confused. Many times a wayward child makes them feel guilty, like they must have missed something.

I don't remember who first pointed it out to me, but this proverb is not a promise. It is a principle. God is telling us that if we do our level best to instill wisdom and right values into a child, they will be more likely to exercise personal freedom in favor of it. Your job is to train, to influence choice.

But the principle implies lots of deviation from "the way." Training children how to live means they certainly will depart from the path, and often. Every fork in the road— whether to lie to mom when I'm not forced to be truthful, to use profanity when dad isn't around to hear me, to take an absentee note to cover skipping school—represents a choice.

Kids will lose their way when given a choice. You hope they will stay on the trail you trained them to take. They may not. As the proverb says, it might take years to change that pattern. Eventually, sometimes not until a child gets quite old and mom and dad are gone, that child makes a comeback to the course learned years before. Our job as parents is to train them in the right way to live, and to do so with the awareness we are helping children walk the tightrope between limits and freedom. If we position them so they can choose wisely, leveraging the tension instead of fighting it, we will have trained well.

Can I be honest? What I see in a lot of parents is a desire to control their kids rather than train them. The older they get, the more desperate the battle of wills gets, because parents want children to play within the limits they instill, but the child pushes everything to the limits of freedom. Control will never be the answer. Instead, you will be doing a balancing act, teetering between the extremes of limits on one side and freedom on the other.

You experience it with your children at various points along the way to their adulthood. When your son or daughter moves from a tricycle to a bike, there is an in-between stage when they need to ride with some help. Sometimes dad holds the seat, limiting the disastrous effects gravity will have on an untrained child. Some kids pick up the training quickly, but most need the help of something to limit the number of times they fall: training wheels. They are needed until that little boy or girl can deal with all the dynamics of two wheels instead of three or four. When they are ready, training wheels come off, and they are a little freer. They can now roam a neighborhood. Even then, they will still fall from time to time. And they are not ultimately free. They can't fly, or go beyond a certain speed because there are still limits.

You see it in a training environment like a classroom, which is a controlled place with limits. Not only are there four walls, but there is a teacher who dictates the basis and pace of learning. But it's an environment where a student gets trained in skills they will put into practice when they leave the classroom and go out into a world of freedom. The training will help them make right choices, like how to play well with others, read and follow directions, and schedule time for varied activities, to name a few. But in the end a student decides what to do with what the teacher offers, and ultimately takes it in or rejects the learning.

44

I like how Henry Cloud and John Townsend describe some of this process in their book *Boundaries with Kids*:

> As a rule, children don't know what they are doing. They have little idea how to handle life so that it works right. That's why God gave them parents—to love them, give them structure, and guide them into maturity. So, just as a puppy needs obedience training, kids need help from the outside. Basically, children will mature to the level the parent structures them, and no higher.[9]

Training wheels, classrooms, and puppies. These are metaphors for real life. A child has to be trained. When a child is taught about freedom and limits, they find out about a tension they will live with as long as they function in this world. The tightrope is ultimately theirs to walk, because effective living requires the right combination of limits and freedom. That's why children have to be trained on how both work.

Limited Freedom and Freeing Limits

Staying on the tightrope strung between limits and freedom requires parents to confront five dynamics they must keep in tune. Just like the strings on a guitar, though, each one will require occasional adjustment if we are going to keep everything in tune with the demands of completing the training challenge. They are:

1. Modeling the behaviors you want your kids to see, imitate, and reproduce
2. Instructing them on the standards and structures that represent your expectations
3. Coaching children with an eye to observation and supervision

4. Correcting the mistakes and attitudes that are in need of tweaking
5. Embedding your ultimate values, so your kids truly own what they have learned

Each of these activities will foster a learning environment where limits become something kids choose. The process will occur, nonstop, for every day of at least the eighteen years between their birth and the legal age for liberation. Tension will be the common theme at every point.

Modeling

Modeling refers to what you do in addition to what you say. The training starts before we say even one word.

One current debate with our boys is over motorcycles. Every parent we know has a firm limit on this issue. It's simple. It is no. Never. Not as long as you live in this house. Many adolescents dream of motorcycles, but the typical parents' refusal leaves little controversy for most homes.

It's not so easy in ours. Since before they can remember, our sons have watched both mom and dad ride off into the sunset dressed in the full getup: leather jackets, fringed gloves, and protective chaps. Darth Vader looked pretty normal compared to the helmeted father figure they have grown up with. Most of the time they were like little Darth Jrs., because they have been riding as passengers since before they could ride nonmotorized bikes. From the time our boys were young, motorcycle touring was our preferred vacation travel mode.

Before the kids could safely climb on the seat behind me, Lynn loved riding "two-up," as bike fanatics call it, as a passenger. Soon, she had to fight the boys for travel time. We talked to fellow riders about our dilemma, and soon an idea emerged. If we latched a sidecar onto a bike Lynn would drive, everyone could ride together—Phil behind me, Mark behind Lynn, and Tim in the sidecar. Lynn cried tears of joy when I drove her birthday gift into the garage (yeah guys, I am a lucky man!), a 1989 Honda Goldwing with a Hannigan sidecar. It was a beautiful moment!

Until Tim outgrew the sidecar, the next five years meant long trips seeing the country the way God meant it to be seen, at least in our opinion. Why drive on four wheels when you could be on two, or if you have to, three?

For Lynn and me, motorcycles are not just recreation, they are in our blood. For our boys, biking—the motorized, faster-the-better version—is not a wish, it is a right. We can refuse, but we are on the losing side of our own modeling.

Fortunately for us, our state's laws postponed our decision to age eighteen, and we're still as scared to death as most parents are of seeing their child risk motorcycle riding. But what do you do when you've modeled something as normal, even good? You have trained your children.

What happens if you say one thing and do another? Your kids will follow what you do. You can say all day long, "Do what I say, not what I do," and they will do what you do. Sometimes that will be positive, because your children will see someone making life choices the right way. That's what you hope for. But we don't always see the implications of our own behavior.

For example, if you want to teach moderation but your kids know you get intoxicated regularly, they will probably do what you do. If you want them to be wise with money but you don't budget, they will follow your cues not your words. If you want them to steer clear of pornography but you won't, they will likely indulge too.

You can try to hide your choices. It may work. But you will lose the moral high ground you need in order to speak authentically into children's lives when you instruct, coach, correct, and try to embed values you hope they choose.

Frankly, this is the hardest part of training; we can think that, because we have told our kids something, they should get it; but that is only part of the equation. You are also a model, often the model after which they will pattern a lot of their behavior.

Instructing

Instructing involves moving beyond what your kids see to what they hear. You have to give them verbal descriptions of what you expect. That may seem obvious. But we forget in the heat of parenting how clear we need to be.

From time to time I talk to a frustrated parent who is blowing off steam over a child's behavior. To understand the issue, I'll ask for one detail, "What did you tell them you expected?" or "Did you tell them X?" I can't begin to count the number of times the response tells the story. Mom or dad was not all that clear.

I can't begin to count how often I'm not clear. My failure to verbalize what I expect from Phil, Mark, or Tim is often the problem when I've been frustrated by something they have done. That doesn't mean all the blame is mine, because they usually have some intuition about what behavior is acceptable, but fuzzy parameters require them to navigate the limits-freedom tightrope. And they can't get off the hook by claiming I was vague when I wasn't (a favorite excuse for bad choices, I've found). But more times than I and parents whose paths I have crossed want to admit, we have missed the demanding chore of simple instruction. In fact, the better the descriptions we give our kids, the more effective our instruction will be.

My friend Dick Anderson had a dad who was good at clarity. When Dick would make a bad choice, his dad would ask a simple question, "Were you thinking?" Dick would start to answer with an explanation of why he did something, such as, "Well, I wanted to . . ." or "Well, Bobby and Jim said we should . . ." or "Well, we figured that . . ." ("Well," is a child's code for buying time for excuse formulation). But his dad would interrupt him with the same question, "Were you thinking?" Further excuses meant another interruption from his dad, "I asked you, 'Were you thinking?' not 'What were you thinking?'"

Dick's dad would not give up until he got the answer he was looking for. When Dick would admit he wasn't thinking, his dad would respond, "That's the problem; you have to think." His insistence on clarity was a springboard for further training for his kids on the way they should go. I've never seen Dick depart from it—he thinks about life and his choices better than most people I know.

Verbal precision matters when we describe our expectations. Consistent, stated principles and values will encode your influence over a daughter or son's later choices. Take a moment to think about how often as an adult you explain your choices with, "You know, my mom (or dad) always told me . . ." The words we speak have power for our kids' entire lives. I've seen simple statements such as, "You have to be kind," "You can do whatever you set your mind to," "Never look down on anyone," "Don't give up too easily," "Don't forget to pray," "Roll with the punches," "Things will look better in the morning," "Work hard, play hard," and scores of other phrases become an encrypted set of instructions that shape a lifetime of choices.

Stated expectations permit you to reinforce what you see in children as well. If you can catch them doing something right or even intercept bad behavior, repetition of your instruction becomes part of the training mix. Never assume a child gets it. It is not a bad idea to use good questions, such as "Have I been clear?" or "What did you hear me say?" as barometers of whether instructions have gotten through.

The instruction task won't get easier as children grow up. I spent seven years in a law firm with Dick McGee, a sixtysomething guy with a curmudgeonly but big-hearted demeanor, and his thirtysomething son, Rick. Rick put his dad and mom through a spin cycle of chaos for a long time. I can't recount most of the stories due to promises of confidentiality!

Dick and Rick eventually got through the wild part of the ride and negotiated the complexities of adult family life and business partnership. When I would relate some of my early parenting woes to Dick and ask him how he got through the tough years with Rick, he would always respond, "Never stop talking to them. They're listening even when they're pretending not to."

To this day, Lynn and I tell each other, "It is Dick McGee time." That is code for us to say it, say it again, say it even though we're sick of hearing ourselves say it. We'll find out later from our kids it was true: they were listening, even though we were getting the stonewall treatment from them.

Instruction applies to a wide range of topics. It can be as simple as prescribing table manners, as complex as proper relational interaction, as significant as appropriate sexual conduct. Sometimes you will instruct because you intercept bad behavior and confront it, other times because you see another family's error and apply what you want to avoid in yours, or because you learn something new and want to redirect the future choices your kids make.

Parents must instruct. Now, is training complete when we have modeled and taught? No. Often we think that's the extent of training, but there are more important dimensions to staying on the training tightrope.

Coaching

Coaching is a popular term these days. Life coaches help people assess and improve their plans and execute the changes they need. Executive coaches tweak the skills of those reaching for the next rung on the corporate ladder. Small group coaches monitor and encourage a church's leaders to provide an increasingly effective network of community and care. Coaching, in these ways and more, can be a helpful idea for parents who want to train their children well.

Let's be clear on what this is *not*. A mom or dad shouldn't become the raving and ranting reincarnation of "Da Coach," Mike Ditka, or the frenzied, sideline pacing, arm waving, overly intense, manic, hair-trigger tempered and frazzled icon we typically picture when we hear about coaches.

Think instead of a tennis or dance coach. They come alongside a protégé to get them on track when they lose their way, improve their technique when they're ready for progress, help them recover from any injuries limiting their effectiveness, and encourage them to be at their best because they see their potential. Parents do all these things with children. Coaching is a core practice we must use to stay on the training tightrope.

Parents coach their children on a myriad of behaviors and skills kids need for life. You can model and instruct them on many aspects of growing up well, but that won't complete the job. When it comes to money, children have to be coached. You need to have a systematic approach to train them on giving, saving, and spending practices. Modeling and instructing well will help, but they have to be coached by someone as they actually begin to earn, manage, and pay out money.

They must develop good study and work habits, especially with today's educational and economic realities. Who is going to train those disciplines? Model all you want, say all you can, but if you do not coach them—watching, evaluating, spotting lapses, and the like—they will not fully know how to confront the continuum of limits and freedom they will find at school and work.

Kids need to learn how to cook, do laundry, and clean. As simple as that sounds, I see an increasing number of families who don't do this. Lynn has been the best coach on this I've seen. Our household has been a coaching clinic when it comes to family chores because she has had a systematic approach to jobs from the time the boys were little. By the time they reached adolescence each of them did their own laundry, maintained their rooms (sometimes after much "coaching"—our family is no different than yours), and could prepare balanced

51

meals. Who knows what choices they will make going forward, but they have been well coached on these basic life skills.

One reason the coaching metaphor works is because many players, once their career is done, move into coaching. Almost every child will move on from playing the role of kid to coaching their own sons and daughters. Your coaching will affect generations to come. Are you coaching at your best?

Correcting

I have carved out correcting as a distinct training dynamic because one of the hard parts of parenting is those situations when a child gets it 90 percent right. But as a parent, you know the missing 10 percent makes all the difference in the world, long term. If parents don't work on the last 10 percent, no one will.

Your son might get most of his chores done a lot of the time, but you know there is an underlying streak of laziness that needs to be dealt with if he is going to become the kind of self-starter employers really value. Your daughter is truthful almost all the time, but white lies aren't so pure when certain situations arise, and they're going to come back to bite her eventually. One of your kids treats people well in every situation, except when a couple of certain friends are around, so you know they still haven't figured out all their own convictions.

Correcting has roots in Bill Hybels's teaching on how we live life as children of God. One of his notable sayings is that "ninety-five percent devotion to Christ is five percent short." Hearing that many years ago has kept me on my spiritual growth edge, even in areas where I sense considerable progress. It's easy for that to turn to perfectionism, which is not Bill's intent. Rightly applied, it keeps me looking at my life with a corrective bent; especially because I know how being a few degrees off-line can put me far off the track miles down the road.

It's true with our children too. In the areas I described above, and in many others, 95 percent is 5 percent short. And that 5 percent variable has way more than a 5 percent impact in the long run. A little unresolved anger means a boy becomes an angry old man, eventually. A little greed can become obsession or deception in an unrestrained adult. A little pride will turn into chronic unwillingness to admit wrong, or a grudge-bearing spirit in the body of a grown-up.

The problem with correcting is that parenting is hard enough already. By the time we model, instruct, and coach, we're tired. Going after the deeper, narrower, or subtler issues in a child whom you can see is already turning out to be a good kid is tough and requires great finesse. But I'm finding that, especially as my boys get older and more able to engage, the fine-tuning issues are the territory where parenting has the most interest and, although I won't know it for a long time, significant payoff.

Rodney Piercey, my law partner, has been a fathering mentor to me. Rod and I have spent countless hours unpacking some of my parenting challenges. Since he is about ten years ahead of me, I've often found he has great wisdom, especially when he has described how specific, tenacious correction trained his two boys, Matt and Ken.

Like most sons, his were regular sibling rivals, and sometimes it got out of hand, like a preview to Armageddon. When that happened, Rod did all the training discussed earlier. But he took another step with them. He devoted many hours with the two of them fine-tuning their attitudes and approaches to conflict. Rod would not settle for mere compliance when he insisted they make peace. He corrected them on how to become great brothers to each other down to the last few nitpicks of what he knew would make a long-term, significant difference in how they related to each other. Now that Matt and Ken are older and married, they have a very unique, close relationship rooted in the corrective training their dad gave them.

There are probably a handful of issues you see in your kids that you have to fine-tune. If you're like me, you would rather ignore them and call the training you have done close enough. That really is not an option, though, is it? Ninety-five percent parenting is 5 percent short. Let's do the fine-tuning on the stuff that really matters.

Embedding

Embedding might strike you as an odd term. What is it? Your training is embedded when a child begins to respond automatically with wise choices. They show respect to adults out of habit rather than parental prompting. They balance fun with work on their own, whether at school, chores, or in their job, because they know what is needed rather than because you restrict them. They choose right friends because they learn to discern how people affect them for good and bad. When you see what you have modeled, instructed, coached, and corrected become ingrained in your kids' DNA, you know they have been trained to stay steady on the tightrope between limits and freedom.

Lynn is an artist when it comes to crafts. She is an expert at knitting, sewing, and crocheting, and has experimented with a lot of similar hobbies. Her quilts populate our home and those of many of our friends and her clients.

One customer favorite is known as a "picture quilt." She has created quilts that use photographs to recount twenty-five or fifty years of marriage, birthdays, and other celebrations. When someone orders a picture quilt, Lynn transfers their photos to fabric, and then creatively features them in the array of material incorporated into the quilt top. You can imagine how meaningful it is for someone to unwrap such a novel frame for a lifetime of memories. When they see how their life is a patchwork of wonderful experiences that makes a beautiful tapestry, it is a profound moment. The photos become embedded into the fabric that makes up the whole.

That is what we are after as parents, isn't it? In the myriad snapshots that will tell the story of our children's lives, we want some of them to reflect an embedded set of values guiding their great choices. We hope the training we've given them will help them successfully perform the lifelong balancing act between limits and freedom. Be on the lookout for whether your training is becoming embedded in them.

Begrudging compliance is not enough. We are looking for owners not renters. If all our children do is camp out on an idea as long as we're around, they have not embedded the training. You cannot consider your modeling, instruction, coaching, and correcting complete until there is evidence your guidance has become a part of the fabric.

This training practice is more a telltale sign you watch for than a practice you do. Embedding is the gauge of where you are on the training tightrope. It points you in the direction you may need to go, whether to limit some freedoms or loosen some restrictions. It helps you find out where, when, and how you may have to apply more training, or modify how you are modeling, instructing, coaching, and correcting. Until you see a child has converted outward conformity to inner conviction, they do not yet really know "the way they should go."

What do you see in your kids when you take an honest look at them? Are the key lessons you hope they will use to guide their life choices truly becoming a part of them? How are you doing at embedding your values as a compass for how they navigate life? Where must you at least try to adjust your training so they begin to reflect how you've pictured a life lived well for them?

Teetering Welcomed Here

Feel the tension? If so, good. If your children are going to exercise their freedom to adopt the values you want them to possess, you will feel it most days as you engage in the process of training. Modeling, instructing, coaching, correcting, and embedding will guide a lifetime of choices. Sometimes it will mean more structure, stop signs, and limits, and other times more letting go, loosened reins, and freedom. Your job is to stay on the parenting tightrope, living with the tension. If you do, you are fulfilling one part of the mom or dad job description. You are training children in the way they should go.

It is just one of the tensions, though. Every parent wobbles on the next tightrope, what we might call *the discipline challenge*. Keep walking.

3

Living with the Law of Big

Always end the name of your child with a vowel, so that when you yell the name will carry.

Parents are not interested in justice, they're interested in peace and quiet.[1]

Bill Cosby

I will never forget the fear in her voice. She was a medical doctor in our community who had just been summoned to court by a complaint filed by our local social services agency. It charged her with abuse for spanking her child. In only a few days she had to appear at a preliminary hearing to determine whether she would lose custody temporarily, while a full investigation was conducted. "What should I do?" she asked with desperation, confusion, and terror.

I didn't help her mood much when we first talked. I started asking about how she would handle the adverse publicity to her practice when the news of the charges got out. Up to that point, she had only been thinking about her little boy, but I pointed out that her career and livelihood were at risk. Her anxiety would continue to rise for days to come.

A handprint on her little boy's buttocks triggered the inquiry. State law required suspected child abuse be reported immediately, so a day care worker had to let local officials know what she had found as she changed his diaper. It wasn't the worst suspicious injury she had seen. But someone had struck a toddler hard enough to leave that much of a mark. It could not be ignored. She did what she had been trained to do and made the phone call.

In the coming weeks the details emerged. This mom had indeed spanked her little boy after failed attempts to make him stop misbehaving during a diaper change. After several admonitions, she gave him one last chance to stop or be paddled. When he didn't she spanked him two or three times on his bare bottom.

It complicated matters that her son suffered from a medical condition, verified through an independent pediatrician, which results in more intense and prolonged bruising than most children experience. Mom knew that, but never thought through the implications of it in the moment discipline was needed. She admitted to spanking him occasionally, but according to many witnesses, no more than most parents.

That didn't matter to the social worker who filed the complaint. She was a young, single woman without children. She admitted during a deposition she thought spanking of any kind was wrong, categorically. According to her graduate training, systems of punishment could be imposed so spanking never would be needed. This was only the first of many complaints she thought would be filed against spankers over time. Her opinion was unshakable.

Several months later the judge dismissed the charge, removed social service supervision, and talked frankly with the social worker about what smelled like an anti-spanking crusade. The mother was ordered to attend parenting classes as a precaution but didn't lose custody or professional standing. News reports never leaked due to a gag order.

After returning to my office from the courthouse I sat with the mom, reflecting on her experience. She had lost any sense of the right way to discipline her child. A highly intelligent, well-trained, esteemed professional was totally confused about what was right when it came to punishing her child. So was I.

So are most parents. One aspect of child rearing every parent questions is discipline. When do I punish? What are the right consequences for bad behavior? Should I spank, and if so how much? Will I get arrested if I do, or if I go too far? What is too far? At what age do you stop spanking? Should I just ground a child, whether in a time-out chair or by taking back the car keys? How do I follow through on the timeless parenting threat, "If you don't stop crying, I'll really give you something to cry about"? These are tough questions, aren't they?

And I don't have any answers . . .

Just kidding.

Actually, I don't have answers if you are looking for easy solutions you can simply put to work without fail. That fallacy disappeared long ago, even before the spanking case I defended.

I do have experience tiptoeing delicately on this tightrope, though. I've imposed too little punishment but then gone too far on other occasions. I've dipped into the well of meaningless threats too often, only to discover one of my kids actually behaved well without my promise of imminent doom. I know what it means to go the wrong direction with the wrong technique, and to inadvertently stumble into some idea that extracted obedience when I least expected it. My confusion has shown up regularly.

Being a typical dad, I've been in the same situations you have. While driving someplace on a family vacation with kids bickering at high decibels behind me I have responded just like my father before me, like his father before him, like all fathers naturally do. "If you don't stop it *right* now, I'm gonna *stop* this car and . . ."

Of course, the boys knew I never would. I'm a guy, bent on setting a *Guinness Book* record for travel time. I won't stop for bathroom breaks, so I sure won't stop to impose discipline, especially when I have a dad's magic reach into the backseat. Phil, Mark, and Tim knew not to incite the arm-over-the-seat treatment that became known as "the claw."

The claw worked best in summer, when bare legs were exposed. There is a tender, fleshy spot right behind the knee that a dad can pinch with varying degrees of intensity, a sort of Taser substitute. The interrogation can begin: "Are you going to stop the fighting?""Yes, Dad!" Pinch a little harder, "Are you sure?" "Yeesss!!" Pinch harder still, "Do you know what I'll do if you don't?" "YYEEEESSSSS!" (They didn't, but were seeking pain relief only by this time.)

If the claw catches you, it is game, set, and match.

Over time, they turned it into a game: "dodge the claw." That didn't stop me. Like Professor Gadget, I have those parental eyes in the back of my head, and an arm my kids think can telescope as long as needed to reach them, even in the full-sized conversion van we drove for a while. The claw had never been beaten.

One day Mark was sitting behind me and started fighting with one of his brothers. Initial intervention didn't work. The fighting escalated. After due warning, out came the claw.

Waving and gnawing toward its prey, it finally caught his flesh—I could feel I had just the right amount this time, so this battle would end quickly. I started demanding he stop the fighting. But this time there was no response. So I just pinched harder. No response. The claw went to max pressure . . . and the back of the van erupted in laughter. The upholstery I was pinching wasn't saying a word.

There has been no end to the ridicule since. "Dad, remember the day you grabbed for Mark's leg and got the seat instead?" Laughter all over again. So much for the claw.

Spared Rods and Spoiled Children

Many people think the Bible encourages parents to punish their kids, early and often, and even endorses severe forms of corporal punishment. What does the Bible really say about discipline?

- Proverbs 19:18: "Discipline your son, for in that there is hope; do not be a willing party to his death." This is a life-and-death deal, God says.
- Proverbs 22:15: "Folly is bound up in the heart of a child, but the rod of discipline will drive it far from him." Discipline is essential due to the folly we all know exists in all of us, especially our children.
- Proverbs 23:13: "Do not withhold discipline from a child; if you punish him with the rod, he will not die." Does "the rod" advocate beatings? No! It seems better to consider this a figure of speech for discipline of any kind.

Ken Davis writes about dealing with the folly in his young daughter, when trying to get her to bed one night.

"Go to bed," I told my daughter. She's stalling. "Daddy, does God talk to us?" "Yes, God talks to us," I said. "Tracy, go to sleep. We'll discuss it in the morning." Being a fool, I imagined that would satisfy her.

"No, we must discuss it now!" she yelled back. "God just spoke to me." Before I could frame an appropriate theological response, she added, "He said I could get up!" "Tracy, go to bed," I commanded. "I need a drink of water," she shot back. The verbal sparring match intensified. "You can't

61

have water." "Why?" "You'll wet the bed." "I quit." How do they respond so quickly? Do they have a game plan? Do they pull random thoughts out of thin air? Is this the root of original sin?

But I wasn't whipped yet. "You didn't quit wetting the bed," I countered. "You wet the bed just last night." She was quick: "The cat did that." She said it without hesitation, without blinking. Maybe she's going to be a lawyer. I ignored the opportunity to laugh. Instead, I made my move to protect my authority. "Don't tell me the cat did it," I bellowed. "The spot on your bed was the size of a large pizza. We only have a tiny, little kitty."

"It wasn't our cat," she said. She was a true professional. She was the best. Yes, she was going to be a lawyer. And she was shocked—SHOCKED—that I would not believe her. I held her by the shoulders. "Look me in the eye," I said, "and tell me the truth." Her bottom lip began to quiver. A huge tear welled up in her eye. "I'm sorry, Daddy," she sobbed, "but a big, giant cat took the screen off my window and jumped on my bed. He wet on my bed. Then he jumped back out the window."

Sensing my skepticism, she continued. "He put the screen back on after he left. That's why it's still there." I was speechless. "He was a big cat," she appended during my keeping silent. I was coming to a slow boil. "I can't believe you'd lie to me like this," I scolded. "I want you to go straight to bed, and I don't want to hear another peep out of you." I learned that one from my father.

I could hear her in her bedroom making tiny, little peeping sounds. Then, after a few more moments of precious, lovely silence, a defiant, little voice screeched from the bedroom, "Daddy, I want water and I want it now!" The gauntlet had been thrown down. My parental authority was up for grabs. I had only one option. I called on the hallowed words of parents from across the reaches of time. "If I hear one more word from you," I roared, "I'll come in there and give you a spanking." "When you come," she said, "bring a glass of water."[2]

In that moment, Ken Davis is exasperated. If he doesn't somehow find a way to deal with his daughter, he is going to blow the moment . . . or blow up in the moment. And on top of it all, the Bible warns him to handle this situation with great care: "Don't keep on scolding and nagging your children, making them angry and resentful. Rather, bring them up with the loving discipline the Lord himself approves."[3] Sounds easy, doesn't it?

From the Claw to Mother Nurture

Of course it's not. "Loving discipline" points us to the other end of the discipline continuum: the *nurture* every parent has to inject into the rhythms of their discipline or they will become nothing more than a nag, "a resounding gong or a clanging cymbal"[4] at risk of missing the ultimate target, love.

I have to admit it: I was pretty lousy on nurture, particularly in the early part of my career as a dad. I was trained in the law, in how to tenaciously cross-examine, win the conviction, and seek the ultimate sentence, all without a shadow of doubt. No mere child was going to beat me.

Until beating the punishment drum too often produced diminishing returns. A chronic and uninterrupted flow of retribution became a wearisome drill.

Lynn was much better at nurture. She is a "feeler" by temperament, which offsets my "thinker" bent, and has gifts of encouragement and shepherding. She could be tough when she had to, but her strong suit was engaging, talking, nudging, cajoling, negotiating, influencing.

Her mom had modeled and coached her into becoming a nurturer of the first order. As I made my way into the Gleason family, it didn't take long to figure out why this family possessed such a loving texture. Joanne Gleason was better at nurture than anyone I've met. Lynn's mom had built such a remarkable relationship with her children that none of the five kids could imagine doing anything to let her down. They engaged in some teenage rebellion, to be sure, but not much and not for long. About all it took to intercept the seeds of disobedience was one look of disappointment from her. It was a rare case of nurture doing the discipline.

Things were not quite so easy for Lynn. Nurture was a good tool in her parenting tool kit. But it didn't work quite like her mom's had. Before we passed the toddler stage, she found out our boys were a little more ready to let mom down, and she found herself regularly disappointed. And confused. Why had nurture worked so well for her mom, but wasn't for her? She must be missing something. Was she just a bad parent?

No. It was hard to see in the moment, but looking back we came to a conclusion. While Lynn's mom had the rare gift of being able to nurture her way through anything, she was not typical. And her mother and father, taken together, had balanced each other so nurture wasn't the only means of discipline Lynn experienced. If anything, Lynn's experience validated reality: there was not a "right" way to parent, her mom's or anyone else's. The attempt to employ a one-size-fits-all strategy to discipline will not work.

And Now, Appearing on Tightrope No. 2

Early in the parenting game, I saw discipline as a debate between the hard-liners versus the teddy bears. After a couple of decades of engaging in the multifaceted process of discipline, and seeing for myself that simple, "right" answers are few and far between, I am much more ready to admit to the tension I feel. I might default to the punishment side, just as Lynn defaults to the nurture side. But I live with more questions than answers in many situations.

So what is it? Punishment or nurture? Yes. Both. Equal doses of punishment when it is needed, nurture when it has to be injected. It is another tension producing *and*. It is *the discipline challenge*, and it looks like this:

Punishment ————————————————— Nurture

We all know this diagram pictures only some of the tension. Dig further into the resources, whether from the expert fields of education, psychology, sociology, law, theology (all of which Lynn and I were educated in). The confusion and anxiety grows more. Teachers debate over structured versus open classrooms. Psychologists and sociologists weigh in on irreversible nature and structures of nurture. Law upholds retribution as theology preaches grace.

And then turn to real-life parenting. Suddenly, you are faced with a belligerent child aged two, ten, or twenty. What now? The Parenting Operating Manual didn't tell you about all the extra knobs and buttons you need to adjust to change your child's attitude.

Add to that the wide range of options you have before you when it comes time to discipline a child. Seemingly good resources contradict each other and leave you confused about what really might work. It can even leave you paralyzed, while your son or daughter becomes the inmate in charge of the asylum.

Once we sized up the discipline challenge as polarities we had to manage rather than a problem to which there was an answer, we could hunker down to walk with more delicate balance.

The more we talked to other parents, we started to identify some of the needs we should pay attention to if we were going to endure the pressure of it all. We found at least seven responsibilities we had to take on in the discipline equation. All of them are necessary.

1. Understand Their Temperament

Temperament is that dimension of your child having to do with their natural bents: how they engage their worlds, take

65

in information and process it, make decisions, and interact with people. A lot of our learning about temperament comes from David Keirsey and Marilyn Bates's book, *Please Understand Me: Character and Temperament Types*.[5] It introduced us to the Myers-Briggs Temperament Type Indicator, which identifies natural personality traits out of which every person functions.

Perhaps you've heard people rattling off alphabet-laden conversation, "I'm an ENTJ. What are you?" "Oh, I am an ISFP." "No kidding? So then we're opposites!" I used to feel like I had crossed into foreign territory when I talked to people who had learned the Myers-Briggs lingo I lacked. It did not take much to learn it, thanks to Keirsey and Bates. They put a valuable diagnostic evaluation right in the first chapter of *Please Understand Me* so you can see how you stack up in the four preferences.

When it comes to interacting with people, do you get more energized by Extraversion or Introversion? Do you tend to think about things using iNtuition or Sensation? Are decisions based on Thinking or Feeling? And do you settle things by Judgment (closure) or Perception (staying open and fluid)? Once you understand each of these four preferences, they can be assembled into a startlingly accurate composite profile, so you know if you are an INFP, ENTP, or whatever—there are sixteen possible combinations. Once you know your temperament type, it will answer a lot of questions you have about why everyone else is so weird when you are so normal!

That is the point of knowing about temperament. We are all wired differently, not good or bad. Once you understand some new language to assess and describe those differences, you interact in bridge-building terms rather than chasm-creating ones. It can transform a marriage or even a workplace.

Lynn and I started by applying temperament lessons to our marriage. Lynn is an Introverted, Sensing, Feeling, Judgment type, while I am an Extroverted, iNtuitive, Thinker who also prefers closure (Judgment). So we are near opposites who spent years wondering what was wrong with the other person. Understanding temperaments may have saved our marriage. We could put away the hammers and chisels we were using to change each other. Without this learning, we probably would each have sought to reshape natural attributes in our kids.

Temperament is not just an adult issue. Each child has preferences too. Apply the principles of temperament types to education or parenting, and you may move from feeling befuddled by one of your kids to understanding why they confront their world, their issues, and their parents the way they do.

One of the best supplements to *Please Understand Me* is *Nurture by Nature*,[6] a guidebook to children's temperaments written by Paul Tieger and Barbara Barron-Tieger. Occasionally, when we've felt stuck on a discipline issue with Phil (ENTP), Mark (INFJ), or Tim (ISTJ), we will pull it out to see if it might provide us with a clue on where to go next. Rather than get frustrated by the boys, we're more ready to engage them in constructive ways.

We just attended Mark and Phil's high school open house, in connection with midterm grading. Since it was a "parents only" session where we got to follow their daily schedule and meet all their teachers, I formed some opinions about each of them. I was particularly impressed by Phil's Trigonometry/Pre-Calculus teacher.

Phil, however, is not impressed. When we debriefed about my experience at home, my barest positive comment about his math teacher drew a sneer from him. "I have a real problem with him," Phil said.

Once upon a time I would have argued the point or tried to persuade him that he ought to like every teacher. Been there, done that. Didn't work. So instead, I simply asked him why, partly to hold myself in check. "I hate math teachers," he responded. "They all believe in rules."

Remember his temperament type? ENTP. The theme for an ENTP child is this: "Everything's negotiable." Rules are made to be broken, and something is wrong if they are not.

We might have spent a lot of years trying to punish Phil into our image of compliance, especially Lynn, the polar opposite ISFJ who values rule keeping, tradition, authority, dependability, and responsibility above all else. All we would have had to show for it was massive parenting stress. Understanding our and his temperaments moved us from punishment to nurture, so we could engage him more constructively.

Instead of getting mad at Phil's defiance toward a good teacher, I could accept a statement that fit completely with his view of our world, laugh in delight at how consistently he reflects his wiring, and engage him in a discussion about how he can continue to function in a world of rules and authority in those settings where limits are unavoidable. Understanding temperament saved not only our sanity but also Phil's life!

2. Learn How They Learn

Each child's temperamental preferences affect your discipline choices. So does each child's unique learning style. There are a variety of views on this subject, but Don Cousins simplified it most for me.

We had a mutual friend seek our advice on something, but were not sure he would accept our counsel. We could not imagine why not, sages that we were! Don described well why he might go his own way rather than do what we recommended. "People learn one of three ways," he explained, "by observation, intuition, or pain." Aha. Our friend only learned through pain. He often cut his own path because it took pain—finding out for himself even if it was the harder way—to teach him.

Don's simple categories have helped us be students of our kids, to understand how they recognize right and wrong. We could then shape them based on their learning style and move along the discipline tightrope in ways that fit them.

All three styles live in our house. Tim is an intuition guy. His instincts about right and wrong are exceptional. Mark learns by observation. Since he is two years younger than Phil, who learns best through pain, he has seen plenty to learn from.

Intuition and observation learners benefit more from tilting a little to the nurture side, while a pain learner *needs* the sting of punishment. You cannot be static and won't be able to treat all your children the same.

You will not be able to respond to one child the same all the time, either. While a child who learns by intuition may have a behavioral pacemaker like Tim, taken too far they become unduly compliant pleasers. Since that will hurt them in the long run, your stay too long on the nurture end of the tightrope may prove unwise. But don't jump to punishment too quickly. You may just be lucky enough to have a non-pleaser, compliant child! So what is the right answer? Learning style differences will keep you off balance as long as there are children to be disciplined.

3. Focus More on Character than Conduct

Author Erwin McManus describes part of the discipline challenge as moving from the realm of mere behavior to the deeper level of character.[7] Jesus described it by looking at a tree: "By their fruit"—behavior—"you will recognize them"—character.[8] Behavior is merely a symptom of what is true on the inside. Character drives all a person is and therefore does. So character must be shaped.

I think McManus is right. We can and need to influence behavior, but forming character is the bigger challenge. We all know this when it comes to children, but often we are content with momentary obedience. Why? It is the expedient approach. By the time parents get up, rush kids off to school, go to work, walk the dog, do the dishes, clean the house, wash the car, go to the bank, help at school, mow the lawn, buy the groceries, cook the meals, make the repairs, pay the bills—all in the first hour of the day due to all the other stuff to be done—who has time to look at trees and fruit? Even more, how do we get the character formation job done?

When we sensed that the fruit ripening on the character tree was turning bad, we called a time-out to get some help. As our kids got older, discipline dynamics got tougher and character issues got deeper. We were stumped on where to turn. So one day Lynn struck on an idea: family counseling. All five of us went to see someone who could help us all.

We ended up in the waiting room of a Christian counselor who had helped numerous families like ours. At first it was like pulling teeth to get responses from early adolescents. His skill won out though, and over time we were able to talk as a family about the deeper issues driving our behaviors.

One of his suggestions: use work to shape attitudes and character. For example, if a child barely completes a chore only after much prodding from mom and negativity from them, add another chore even harder than the first. It will only be considered finished when it is done with a positive attitude. If that does not shift attitudes, try a third or fourth chore until something moves *inside the child's heart*.

We tried it a few times. It wasn't like magic, but over time we saw some shifts in mind-set. Jobs became part of the discipline repertoire, a tool we could use to respond in those moments where character was showing up as the deeper issue.[9]

You might not need to call someone like we did. You may not need to use work as a means to change attitudes. But adjusting your discipline focus to zero in on character might help you walk the discipline tightrope more effectively.

4. Be Objective

We all have heard stories about parents who rush to their child's defense when he or she has been caught doing something wrong. They feel personally offended when their son or daughter has been wrongly accused, at least in their view.

The only problem: everyone else knows what their kid has been up to, and it's about time they got caught. Mom and dad have lost objectivity.

Maybe more painful is the parent who has lost the ability to see *good* in their child; rather than nurture seeds of positive growth, that parent keeps the hammer down. Losing objectivity either way will knock you off the tightrope.

That would never be you or me, though. We see things clearly at all times, right?

Lynn and I used to think we did, until we moved into the more intimate community of a small group. As our discussions got a little more personal, parents started sharing their confusion over discipline questions. Over time we all felt a sense of increasing safety. Soon we could start to tell each other what we saw in each others' parenting and children. We could see our unduly positive or negative outlook toward our kids through some other lenses. It turned out that our occasionally rose-colored glasses needed a new prescription, and clouded vision needed clarity.

When we started the parenting voyage, we thought it was largely a solo one. Not! It is fair game to get input from those around you. When it comes to discipline, most of your family and friends have opinions on how you—and your kids—are doing anyway. You might as well ask others what they see.

They might help you spot something you've missed, correct wrong thinking, or give added insight. You might even find out you are a whole lot better parent than you think!

5. Vary Your Techniques

Henry Ford used to say of the Model T, "You can have it in any color you want, as long as it is black." During my growing up years, it seems like spanking was the black paint of Model T parental discipline.

That is not intended to be as critical as it sounds. My mom has reflected frequently on how few good resources parents had when she and my dad were trying their best to raise us. So they did unto others as was done to them. Spanking was the universal solution when discipline had to be imposed. We had a permanent campsite on the punishment end of the tightrope.

I would have started out the same way if it wasn't for Lynn. Since she held degrees in both Christian education and elementary education, her understanding of child development was better rounded than mine. She pushed us to be more creative, which in turn brought better balance to our discipline. We used spanking and time-out chairs regularly, but also worked hard to make the punishment match the crime.

For example, we lived in a tri-level home when the boys were growing up; add in the basement, and we had four sets of stairs. We also had three little boys who sometimes got into trouble due to an excess of testosterone. When they needed some discipline, burning off some of that energy along the way made it all the more effective. So running stairs became a part of the regular punishment mix. Our kids will never exercise on a StairMaster because it brings back the dreaded memory of running fifteen or twenty sets of stairs, top to bottom, at age five or six. But it sapped some of the energy young boys used to attack each other, so it worked for us.

Maybe your children bicker like ours did. It was annoying for us and collided with a core value we wanted to put into the fabric of their relationship, to be good brothers to each other. So we decided to intercept squabbling early, which also meant often. What punishment fit that offense? We imposed a system to let them know if they couldn't get along, then they could spend some time apart.

It worked like this: if they could not resolve a quarrel after some reasonable attempts, it meant both kids—and sometimes all three of them—went to their bedrooms for five minutes, doors closed, no electricity (since a radio, stereo, Game Boy or the like could ease the pain). After five minutes, they could reengage, but when the next bickering session started, it was

72

another bedroom session, but this time for ten minutes. Each additional, same-day, unresolved clash added another five minutes. By the time they hit the twenty- or twenty-five minute round, they started to figure out they better get along, or they would end up with very dull days during their elementary school years.

They were tough, though. I remember one day when all three of them hit the thirty-minute round, which meant they each were in isolation for 105 minutes that day. We sure enjoyed the serene environment. They decided to be better brothers to each other because of the incentive to negotiate their differences.

What do you do when fights turn physical? As our guys got older, they occasionally skipped verbal argument in favor of an odd but violent blend of WWF wrestling, Ninja Turtle martial arts, and nasty street fighting. It seemed pretty routine to me, but Lynn grew up mostly around girls, so she was scared to death. A family counseling session in which we talked through her fear with Phil, Mark, and Tim produced a fresh thought. If the boys wanted to turn their conflicts into physical warfare, they had to use boxing equipment. They agreed it could be a less dangerous way to channel their anger, since they didn't particularly like the bruising produced by their method.

It cost me fifty dollars at a local sporting goods store to buy the gloves and headgear, and then it never got used. It was money well spent, though, because the threat of either being hit by an older, bigger brother, or being humiliated by a younger, more aggressive sibling, would back them down. The time it took them to go get the gear, put it on, and initiate the match gave them time to decide whether their issues were worth fighting over. They usually decided to throw in the towel.

Some of you might be tempted to view these varied techniques as magical answers. Don't. That would be dot-to-dot discipline. Try these if you like. But in the end, do what works, what seems in your family to strike a better balance of punishment and nurture. It requires a lot of experiments on how to impose punishment, but it's worth it when you find something that strikes a balance and works for your family.

6. Play to Each Parent's Strength

Over the years, Lynn and I have devoted many hours to conversation with Andy Hartman, another skilled Christian counselor with an office near us and a phone seconds away. He not only helped us find individual healing for what ailed us on the inside, but he also kept our marriage together when we had to deal with what would break it. We have reached twenty-eight years in a marriage better than it has ever been, thanks to God, Andy, and a lot of hard work and sheer resolve.

Andy advised us with great wisdom on how to discipline our kids more effectively too. One key suggestion: take advantage of having both of us as parents.

That said, I write with an acute awareness of the unique challenge some of you face as single parents, because most of the time it is a solo deal. After countless hours with single parents, sometimes in law offices, mediation sessions and courtrooms, other times in prayer as an elder, counseling as a pastor, or discussion as a small group leader, I see that the tightrope you walk is incalculably more difficult. Single parents who fight through their parenting challenges alone are some of the bravest people I know.

Walking with single parents has reinforced the advice Andy Hartman gave us: when you do have the benefit of two parents in a home, it makes sense to take advantage of it.

Lynn is a lot better than I am at dealing with feelings and offering encouragement, and I am best when formulating solutions and facilitating decisions. For a long time, we thought we both needed to be engaged when discipline was needed. Once we felt permission to ebb and flow the punishment and nurture to and from the parent who could best meet the need, we found better equilibrium.

74

This also extends to individual children. Lynn has often been better working with Mark, due to his temperament and tendency to be easily bruised when he was younger. Frankly, I was too blunt an instrument sometimes! I have been better with Phil, because he and I are wired similarly, and I can almost predict how he will respond most times because I approached life so similarly at his age. Tim's needs vary more by situation, but we try to take turns based on who will serve him best in the moment. We stay united on discussing the process needed and outcomes hoped for, but divide and conquer in the engagement.

We play to each others' physical presence as well. There are times when even big boys need their mom's touch. She still likes to cuddle them even when they turn prickly these days. And she loves nothing better than those moments when touch and time creates deep and nurturing conversation, soul to soul.

Lynn would rather live in the land of nurture, but then I have to remind her: there are plenty of times you can't just talk these guys into doing the right thing. They have to understand what my friend Doug Veenstra calls the "Law of Big." That is where I come in. I can *be* the Law of Big. When the need arises to back down an aggressive attitude, confront bad behavior with adult force, or impose punishment on a late adolescent, I become the wall they need to run into. I let Phil, Mark, and Tim know I can still take them out even as a graying, less spry forty-eight-year-old. So far they haven't tested the wall.

To this day, we keep them guessing over how we play to our strengths. So Lynn and I discuss when we should do a role reversal in the moment, or even in the mood—when one of us is simply too tired or preoccupied to discipline effectively. Don't get too predictable. We take turns being the good cop and bad cop, since both of us can play.

Let me circle back to single parents. If you are battling the discipline challenge alone, you may want to do what other single parents do. They lean on grandparents or siblings, build a network of parents with similarly aged kids who bring different strengths, and take advantage of a church with small groups for junior high and high school students. In the end, this is not the only means through which you can stay on the discipline tightrope. You can still understand temperament, learn how they learn, focus on character, be objective, and vary techniques. You will need all of these, and then some, to keep from teetering too much.

7. Never, Never, Never, NEVER Give Up

The final suggestion: be tenacious. Conceding defeat is not an option. The day you give in is the day you have swapped roles with your child. When your behavior is triggered by theirs, you adapt to their choices, and they are now in charge.

I can't begin to tell you the number of times—especially as our kids approach adulthood—I have wanted to give up. There are days when, out of utter exasperation at surviving another fruitless round of trying to shape behavior, I want to say, "OK, you want it your way? Have it your way. I will give in just to let you experience the results of bad choices. Then you will know." But then another phrase interrupts. Winston Churchill said it to a war-weary nation. "Never, never, never, never give up."[10]

You are the parent. Your job is not to be popular with your kids. Your job is to discipline them. Will you have the internal strength to undergo possible rejection by your children? Discipline demands it.

Sometimes that will mean moving into increased punishment, and they will hate your guts. Sometimes it will mean breaking through their hard shell to keep nurturing touch and conversation going, even when it feels awkward. But parachuting off the tightrope won't work any better than living too long on either end of it.

Some parents will say, "Well, they are eighteen now, so what can we do?" I know because I have said it. I found an answer. Plenty. I still own the door to the house, the keys to a car, and the easiest ticket to college. I cannot employ them capriciously, because after eighteen years of parenting, my kids know me as well as I know them.

They know I want them around home until it is time for them to get on with their life, that I hope they get a great education, and that I aspire for them to be remarkable adults who make a mark in our world. They also know I will put those things on the line if I see how uncorrected behavior will serve them worse than no bed, no car, or no degree. I have had to figure out which appropriate forms of punishment I can still exercise (see chapter five for more here), while doing my level best to keep a nurturing undertone. I won't give up no matter how tough the battle gets.

My children haven't turned away from me, at least not yet. They haven't turned *on* me, either. I have friends whose kids have. They were tenacious, even walked the tightrope with what I judged to be great deftness. In the end, a son or daughter rejected not only the discipline, but the parents too. What should parents do when sound discipline has turned sour, and how do they fight off feelings of guilt, confusion, and sorrow?

I think in those moments we all have to go where God does. When we as his children choose rebellion over submission, the Bible tells us he is saddened by our willfulness. He gets angry when we won't do the right thing and yet continues doing what he can to draw us back in. In the end, though, he leaves our free will in play, so we choose to love and obey him, which becomes the foundation for a relationship characterized by autonomy. He sticks by the truth, so we become free.

Ironic, isn't it? We have to insist on right and wrong, outline rules and privileges, and choose punishment and nurture, only to let our children go into a life independent of it. The years of discipline will go with them, though, when they use their freedom to choose it for themselves.

Leaving the Guesswork In

Between wherever you are today and the day you find out how your children respond to your discipline, you will be on a tightrope. There will be no easy answers, just many answers you will have to decide how to apply in your situation. Sure it will mean some guesswork. But if you embrace the tension, stay sensitive to where you should adjust your approach, and tweak your thinking along the way, the discipline challenge will become less confusing.

Be a student of your child and zero in on their temperament, how they learn, and the reality of where they are developmentally. Stay objective, vary your techniques, and play to your strengths as best you can. And never, never, never, NEVER give up.

Getting used to the tension? Good. Because *the spiritual challenge* is about to throw you off kilter.

4

Don't Tell Me *That* Old, Old Story

The Spiritual Challenge

On their way to church one Sunday evening, a couple's six-year-old daughter blurted out, "Mommy, do you and Daddy have sex?" Before they could say a word, their eight-year-old son shot back, "Of course not! They're good Christian people."[1]

Liz Curtis Higgs

"Daddy and I walked along a pathway beside the lake," recalls Franklin Graham, namesake of evangelist Billy Graham. "My father, who hates confrontation, turned to me and, somewhat nervously, said: 'Franklin, your mother and I sense there's a struggle going on in your life.'"

In his autobiography, *Rebel with a Cause*, Graham continues the story about a memorable walk with his dad along the banks of Lake Geneva, Switzerland.

I stared at him, but I didn't say anything. He had caught me totally off guard. *How does he know this?* I wondered.

"You're going to have to make a choice either to accept Christ or reject Him. You can't continue to play the middle ground. Either you're going to choose to follow and obey Him or reject Him."

My mind raced. *What was he going to say next?*

"I want you to know we're proud of you, Franklin. We love you no matter what you do in life and no matter where you go. The door of our home is always open, and you're always welcome. But you're going to have to make a choice."

I felt angry. Maybe I was mad because he had seen right through me. I'd always thought I was so clever and could fool my parents. After all, I went to church, sang the hymns, and said the right words. But my sinful life was not secret. I couldn't figure out how he knew about the struggle that had been going on inside me for some time. But he did. I knew he was right.

After he had his say, Daddy patted my shoulder and smiled. He said nothing more about it as we finished our walk.

But in spite of some of the most beautiful and inspiring scenery in the world—and near the man I loved and wanted to please more than anyone else on earth—I felt joyless, empty, lonely, and dirty. The clock was ticking loudly now on my own personal "hour of decision."[2]

Billy Graham had poignantly captured the essence of Franklin's twenty-two-year struggle over what to do with his famous parents' faith. Decades of unnamed tension were bubbling to the surface.

The words of my father a few weeks earlier haunted me: "Franklin, you are going to have to make a choice to accept Christ or reject Him." I thought back to the time I had made a decision for Christ at age eight. I'm not sure I really understood what I had done. All I know was that Franklin Graham was a sinner who had been running from

80

God. Suddenly, I had an overpowering conviction that I needed to get my life right with God.

I read John 3 again where Jesus told Nicodemus, "You must be born again." Nicodemus was a respected religious leader in his city. Yet all of his religion and learning were not enough to gain entrance into heaven. Nicodemus had to be born again. All I knew was that I wanted the big empty hole inside of me to be filled. I was tired of running. . . .

I put my cigarette out and got down on my knees beside my bed. I'm not sure what I prayed, but I know that I poured my heart out to God and confessed my sin. . . .

That night I finally decided I was sick and tired of being sick and tired. My years of running and rebellion had ended.[3]

And with that, two parents—Billy and Ruth Graham—saw a happy ending to a difficult story they had watched unfold in their oldest son's life. Not only did Franklin make his choice, he continued to walk with his dad into Christian leadership, founding World Medical Mission, guiding Samaritan's Purse, and eventually succeeding his father as head of the Billy Graham Evangelistic Association.

The Grahams' story inspires hope in parents with sons or daughters in rebellion against what their family has stood for spiritually. Moms and dads wear out their knees praying spiritual rebellion will turn soon. Sometimes there is a payoff. Other times? Chronic helplessness and heartbreak . . . and nonstop tension.

Fighting Spiritual Forgetfulness

The Bible hands parents the responsibility to maintain spiritual momentum in a family. It starts in the Old Testament with Deuteronomy 4:9: "Watch yourselves closely so that you do not forget the things your eyes have seen or let them slip from your heart as long as you live. Teach them to your children and to their children after them." God knows how forgetful we are of life's spiritual lessons. So he counsels us to fight off forgetfulness and never leave kids in a place where they have to learn spiritual lessons the hard way—by turning their back on God and their own spiritual need. He also knows children are watching to see what your spiritual life is like and how you connect with God.

One word for it is *tradition*. Tradition (custom, ritual, habit, beliefs, routine, convictions are other synonymous ideas) is a term that has fallen into disrepute. We hear about tradition, and it evokes the image of Tevye in *Fiddler on the Roof*:

> A fiddler on the roof. Sounds crazy, no? But here, in our little village of Anatevka, you might say every one of us is a fiddler on the roof trying to scratch out a pleasant, simple tune without breaking his neck. It isn't easy. You may ask, "Why do we stay up there if it's so dangerous?" Well, we stay because Anatevka is our home. And how do we keep our balance? That I can tell you in one word: tradition![4]

Tevye's daughters teach him—and all of us—how tradition, while good, leads to imbalance when it preoccupies the spotlight. The generation following Tevye ultimately finds his spiritual tradition worthy of consideration, but only after they are given some space to figure out how it fits into their world.

We hate to admit it, but if it takes dancing on rooftops to see our kids incorporate our spiritual convictions, routines, and beliefs into the fabric of their lives, we will do it. We harbor deep hopes they will opt for the same spiritual path we've taken. Is that bad? Not at all. The spiritual tradition you establish for your home is not only good, but a required duty for parents to fulfill their responsibility to their children, and to God.

You see the benefits of parents who pass on their spiritual legacy throughout the Bible. Despite ups and downs along the way, Isaac takes the baton from Abraham, and God extends his promise to use their family to change human history. Esther is positioned to become the queen who saves her nation from genocide. How? Because both her parents and an uncle named Mordecai kept her focused on God's purposes for her life, so she could be prepared "for such a time as this."[5] Paul urges his young protégé, Timothy, to continue his course of faithfulness by reminding him of his family's spiritual trend line: "I have been reminded of your sincere faith, which first lived in your grandmother Lois and in your mother Eunice and, I am persuaded, now lives in you also."[6] I've never forgotten words one of my Bible college teachers once said, "It takes a family like Timothy's to produce a Timothy." It is the dream parents understand.

But we also know it is no simple process to help children reach their "hour of decision." Perhaps you have heard of the old Sunday school teacher who asked her young students, "What is brown, has a big tail and collects nuts?" After a moment of silence, a regular attender piped up. "Sounds like a squirrel to me," the little boy said tentatively, "but I am going to answer, 'Jesus!'"

Tradition can become a rote conformity that turns spiritual momentum into legalism or, even worse, a subtle form of brainwashing. Small doses of mere religion can act as a spiritual immunization shot, shielding a child from being fully infected with the transforming love of Christ.

Taking the Long Way Home

Children who become resistant to the full dose of Christianity infuriate, confuse, and break the hearts of parents who deeply value their own spiritual convictions and customs. Any mom or dad who has given their heart and life to Christ—especially if they can attest to their own former sense of emptiness or futility—wants to spare anyone they know from even a moment of emptiness and futility.

But the Bible fully describes the other end of the continuum, a son or daughter's private choice, even though, when a child makes matters of belief their own, they may go astray.

One of the best examples is Jesus's story of the prodigal son.[7] Jesus tells of two brothers, one compliant and one rebellious. The rebellious one asks his father for early inheritance, so he can get out of the house. The dad agrees, apparently knowing this kid has to learn the hard way. The son does learn, eventually. After considerable pain he decides to see if his dad will permit reconciliation. He returns to a dad who has been waiting for him to take the long way home.

The reunion with the father is not only a happy ending to that story; it is one of the best pictures of what it looks like for us to go from being prodigal sons and daughters to reconciled children of our heavenly Father. Jesus says the dad in this parable is just like God, who at every moment is scanning the horizon for returning rebels who have scoped out the other options and found out they won't meet needs humanity can only gratify by spiritual means. When the prodigal returns, there are waiting, open arms prepared to forgive and forget.

God's amazing grace, and the prodigal's loving reception upon returning home, only adds to our confusion as parents. When children exercise their spiritual choice to run the opposite direction of their parents, we would like to prevent it. But we cannot.

When kids reject our spiritual roots, we're not alone. You see kids like the prodigal son through the whole Bible, starting with Genesis. Cain kills his brother, Abel, and by all indications lives away from his family for the rest of his life.[8]

Within two generations of Abraham's profound faith experience, his nephew (and de facto adopted son), Lot, barely escapes Sodom, only to have his daughters initiate the first acts of incest.[9] Generations to come remain spiritually wayward.

84

Eli is one of the godliest men of his day, entrusted with guiding Samuel's spiritual devotion. His sons, Hophni and Phinehas, are another story: "Eli's sons were wicked men; they had no regard for the LORD."[10] Their lives turn into a tragedy for themselves, and their father.

Absalom is the insubordinate son of the man after God's own heart, David.[11] Although he is heir to the throne of God, Absalom rejects his father's guidance, and ultimately plots a coup. He never recovers from his waywardness. His choices leave him dead in battle. Sometimes children who decide to follow the path of the prodigal never make it home.

It is one of the hardest things a parent has to do, but at some point a dad like the one in Jesus's story has to let his child choose his spiritual future. It points every mom and dad to the other end of the spiritual challenge continuum— choice.

Doing Two Good Things at Once

So what do we do?

Should we be consistent about reinforcing our own take on spiritual life? *Yes!* Deuteronomy 6:6–9 tells us the appropriate tone with which to do it:

> These commandments that I give you today are to be upon your hearts. Impress them on your children. Talk about them when you sit at home and when you walk along the road, when you lie down and when you get up. Tie them as symbols on your hands and bind them on your foreheads. Write them on the doorframes of your houses and on your gates.

Parents are supposed to be in nonstop engagement mode when we tend to the spiritual direction of our children. We must have an ever-present influence. We have to.

Should we be patient while our kids make their spiritual choices? *Yes!* Children, like all human beings, have free will. They have to be given room to choose. In fact, perhaps the greatest tension of all time is how to reconcile our free will with God's absolute sovereignty.

Paul writes to one church, "In him we were also chosen, having been predestined according to the plan of him who works out everything in conformity with the purpose of his will."[12] Sounds like the salvation we hope our children will find is all in God's hands, right? But Paul also describes the activism needed if people will decide to follow Christ, "We are therefore Christ's ambassadors, as though God were making his appeal through us. We implore you on Christ's behalf: Be reconciled to God."[13] If the decision has already been made by God, why urge someone to choose reconciliation?

What is the right answer to the divine sovereignty/human choice tension? I'm no theologian, but I know enough Greek and hermeneutics to have studied the issue to the point that I wonder if it is both. Paul seems to be at peace reflecting on dual truths in the mind of God that are best resolved by holding them in dynamic tension. While people have fought wars over the "right" view on election and free will, what if the right answer is to see them as polarities?

Parents, in some ways, are in the same boat as God when it comes to their children's spiritual future. There are times when we would like to superintend their choice "in conformity with the purpose of *our* will" even if it means violating theirs. While God might have that option, he apparently won't exercise it.

As much as both he and we would love to see multiple generations establish a tradition of making fantastic spiritual decisions to walk closely with him, each person is allowed to choose. Most of the time all we can do is implore children to be reconciled to God, and to us, by choosing the path we've chosen. We are on a tightrope once again, which looks like this:

Tradition ——————————————————— Choice

Walking this tightrope will require us to become highly tolerant of tension, so we reinforce all the spiritual guidance needed by each child, while dodging periodic inclinations to push too hard. It will change from child to child and season to season, well into adulthood. There will be few easy answers most of the time. But walking this tightrope is not optional.

How do we foster authentic relationships that will lean into family tradition but leave room for private decision? Some suggest things like nightly family Bible study, structured prayer times, Bible memorization plans, and the like. Lynn and I have tried some of those things, and some of them work some of the time; if those ideas fit your family, do them. Over time, though, I think you will need to do a more elaborate balancing act.

It Takes Partnership

Our family moved to Chicago, Illinois, in 1989. I had practiced law for seven years with a firm in Minot, North Dakota (Lee Strobel's slant on its low population when I landed in Chicago: "Did you turn out the lights when you left?"). Since my Chicago venture was a fresh start, I decided to strike out on my own.

The first day was lonely. One desk, one chair, and one computer in a 15' x 15' office. No clients. It truly was starting from scratch.

Slowly but surely, the clients came. After a couple of years I was able to hire two secretaries, including my mom, who I think may have worked her final few years before retirement for me out of sheer pity! She walked that part of her parenting tightrope like the pro she was.

As things grew, I added two "associates," the label lawyers use to tag younger attorneys, and went through a couple of modest office relocations hedging against unpredictable growth by crimping both size and commitment of space.

There came a time, though, when I had to make a serious leap to take this little law practice into its future as a long-term, more stable enterprise. I finally took one big leap and signed a five-year lease in a first-class building. But if I was going to build this venture into a lasting one, I needed to team up with more than retiring family members, secretaries, and associates, since they can leave at any time, and then I'd only be stuck with a long-term lease obligation and fewer hands for the work. Increased stability required more than people who could leave at will. I needed people with "skin in the game." I needed partners.

A partner is someone who takes on part of the ownership, who helps carry the load of work and financial risk, and who has a much harder time departing the business than non-partners. Partnering with others makes for less loneliness, wiser decisions, and shared celebration in success. Partners are in for the long haul and, if they are good ones, open up fresh possibilities for continuing growth.

Spin the clock forward. Seven partners have teamed up to create a stable firm of thirty employees, one that blesses those who are part of it, our clients, families, and communities included. "Partnering" has become a defining way we do business because of the power created when people see themselves as stakeholders in where we are going . . . together.

Partnering applies to more than businesses. Parents facing the spiritual challenge need partners in the venture of shaping their children's eternities. There is too much at stake to go it alone. You want some others who can share the load, help you spot risks, be ready when it gets lonely, increase wisdom, celebrate the wins, settle in for the long haul, and make the most of every growth opportunity you and your kids will find along the way. Use a partnering approach to the spiritual challenge, and you'll find greater stability on the tightrope.

Partnering with Your Kids

Have you ever thought of your kids as partners in the parenting process? When it comes to shaping their spiritual choices, they can be your allies in ways they might not even know. A lot of it depends on how you understand their "spiritual pathway."

Gary Thomas authored a book several years ago that introduced us to this idea. In *Sacred Pathways*[14] he contests the idea that we all connect with God the same way, such as through traditional quiet times of prayer and Bible study. While that approach might work for some, he cites Scripture, Christian classic literature, church history, and human psychology to show how each of us has one of nine "sacred pathways," patterns of connecting with God we can determine by looking over the course of our lives. Once we figure out our pathway, walking with God becomes more natural and growth-producing.

Thomas identifies people who pursue God via nine pathways:

- Naturalists feel the love of God most when they are outdoors, enjoying his creation. Put a naturalist in a prayer closet, and you have doomed them.
- Sensates are at their spiritual best when all five of their senses are working overtime. A worship experience featuring sound, visual imagery, incense, and their own activity puts them in God's presence.
- Traditionalists love to tap generations of church history and practice to enrich their own small part of it. Liturgy, ritual, and symbols matter to them more than anything.
- Ascetics make spiritual progress when engaged in disciplines such as solitude, silence, and fasting. The more they engage in such practices, the more inclined they are to God.

89

- Activists think there is nothing better than meeting God out on the limb of faith, so they naturally look for him there. Structure or repetition fits them like a straightjacket.
- Caregivers show their love for God by how they love others. No matter how much they give of themselves, they sense nothing but God's love for them in return.
- Enthusiasts move right into God's presence when they can clap, dance, sing, and shout. Thomas calls them "the cheerleaders for God and the Christian life!"[15]
- Contemplatives seek images to transform their spiritual experience. The bigger the picture of God or the sacred, the more they are drawn into it in ways that enrich their personal engagement with the divine.
- Intellectuals must have their mind engaged or they go nowhere fast. Theology, apologetics, study, doctrine; these are the fields in which they can run free and find that God touches their heart, not just their mind.

Your child has his or her own spiritual pathway. For some it is obvious, and as you read the list you are smiling when you spot their preferred means of finding God in the world. Maybe you identify your own just as quickly. It may not be a singular pathway. Thomas's insights suggest some kids will find two or three pathways or move toward God along varied paths from era to era.

That is why you have to partner with them. Pressing children into preferences ill fitted to them will be futile. Playing only to the more traditional, contemplative, or ascetic activities viewed by most as the "right" way to connect with God limits their potential to choose a long-term relationship with him. Presenting your preferred path as better can push them away from God too.

What if you were to team up with your kids to find out how they best relate to God, and help them into it? Despite your own differences with them over spiritual direction, you may come to realize you only diverge on *how* to connect with God.

Learning about spiritual pathways helped us understand how to vary the menu of spiritual experience. For example, we sent our boys to Kamp Kanakuk, Joe White's Christian sports camps in southern Missouri, because we liked their varied approach to helping kids connect the dots in their spiritual life. While there was an appropriate amount of time for worship, study, prayer, and the like—the pathways many of us grew up thinking were the only spiritual methods that counted—they used the outdoors, recreation, relationships, craftsmanship, and other activities as spiritual leverage points with kids of all ages.

We used "pathway language" during debriefing sessions after their two-week experiences. Phil (activist) was most stimulated by the adventure sports, Mark (contemplative enthusiast) enjoyed worship and solitude times, and Tim (intellectual-caregiver) combined all he learned from the teaching with the friendships he formed with leaders and kids to make spiritual headway. When we visited, I (an activist like Phil) wanted a turn on the high ropes course and water slide, while Lynn (naturalist-sensate) was magnetically pulled into the woods for a long, slow walk where she could smell, touch, see, and feel the beauty of the camps.

Finding out about spiritual pathways not only liberated Lynn and me from a narrower, traditional understanding about spiritual life, it helped put concepts and language to our conversations with our children about God. We could better help them choose the path that fit them instead of dictating artificial terms of spiritual engagement.

Sure, we had our personal and family routines and rituals of prayer, church, and all. But we were more cooperative partners with our children's patterns. We knew more about when to throw Phil the challenge of a missions trip or inner-city projects, how to help Mark get started with journaling and blossom as a drummer so he can engage in worship with a very loud instrument, and where to keep Tim intellectually challenged and relationally nurtured. We have not reached the finish line of all their own spiritual choices just yet, but we can see how our preferences and traditions are dovetailing with their own.

Partnering with Each Other

In the same way that children have unique spiritual pathways, parents have unique inclinations on how they will guide them toward God. Just as one-size-fits-all methods won't work in any child-rearing challenge, standardizing your spiritual influence limits your potential to affect their choices for long-term relationships with God.

For example, in our family Lynn has a more daily, routine skill set and presence. She has been the one to insist we keep dinner together a priority. Everyone in our family knows you have one of three choices: (1) be at the table by 6:00 p.m. each day, (2) obtain permission to be gone, or (3) have an awfully good excuse for absence or tardiness. The dinner table has not only become one of our consistent forums for random discussion, it has also emerged as a centerpiece of spiritual conversation and formation.

She has experimented with family devotional routines, which have worked to varying degrees from abject failure to modestly interesting. But she will not give up on it even if we try, swing, and miss.

Lynn is also known to friends and family for voracious journaling and letter writing. She has modeled a daily contemplative bent, which in turn gives our kids permission to regulate their days with an ear to the inner world. When her words find their way to the many notes and letters she has written to Phil, Mark, and Tim, they embed themselves in the recesses of these little boys who are quickly becoming men.

92

Each day seems to bring a new book as well. Lynn keeps everyone intellectually curious, ready to explore whatever question they have about matters of faith. When spiritual questions or debates arise, if she hasn't read about it, she will find the right book to hand off to children who have learned to keep searching for answers to their questions.

Lynn can't help but embed prayer into our family's life (her one-time job as director of Willow Creek's prayer ministry was an outgrowth of her own prayer life). She makes us pause to ask God for safety and blessing before the car goes in gear for vacation travel. She catches prayer times with the boys before they hustle out the door to school whenever she can. Talking to God at every turn, at any time, is a daily routine.

I pray, teach, and model some of what Lynn does too. But my style is not as daily and consistent as Lynn's is. My approach might be described as a sort of "big play" style. For example, once each year I kidnap the guys, one at a time, for a weekend father/son trip. It started the year they turned age three.

They get to pick a destination within a reasonable distance and budget where we will spend a couple of nights together. Over the years we've made baseball pilgrimages to every Midwest stadium we could get to, motorcycle tours that left us with bugs in our smiling teeth and bowed legs when we finally stopped, and music junkets to expand their artistic bents. We have been on boats, planes, trains, helicopters, and racing karts. They compete to come up with new ideas to see what bait their dad will take. They know I'm an easy mark for whatever will capture the imagination.

In the midst of the annual big plays, though, they know our conversation will turn to their spiritual journey. During each trip I introduce a theme based on a proverb or other Bible verse. It starts at age eight, when the lesson for that year is "A good name is worth more than great riches,"[16] so we can talk about the value of integrity. When they are nine years of age, we discuss how "bad company corrupts good morals,"[17] because they need to know God's perspective on how to choose friends. Age ten's trip provides the chance to talk about the significance of what they watch and listen to from music, TV, and movies: "The eye is the lamp of the body."[18] They display both dread and curiosity when we talk about how important it is to "flee youthful lusts"[19]—the sex discussion—at age eleven (Phil and Mark had fun preparing Tim for that trip!). Each year means it is time for another big play. That style fits me well.

The further benefit: during the rest of the year situations arise where one of the lessons applies, and all I have to do is ask, "So what's the proverb, guys?" Sometimes they roll their eyes before they sarcastically reply, "Build others up,"[20] "A fool gives full vent to his anger,"[21] or one of the other relevant verses. I aim to have them leave our home with a dozen guiding ideas, accumulated from age eight to eighteen. My ultimate dream? For their kids to hear them say, 'You know, my dad always used to tell me . . ." They just might choose to heed the guidance in the end because the lessons were learned in the course of goofing off with a dad who taught them if life is not an adventure, it is not worth living!

We are still on the road to finding out what our kids will choose and why. At least they will have seen each of their parents engage them in ways that fit not only them, but us as well.

Partnering with Others

Dave Presher would come to our house in Fridley, Minnesota, every few weeks when I was a kid. He became a good friend not only to me but to my family. It was not because he and I had a whole lot in common. Dave was a rarity—a male babysitter.

He was bright, athletic, and personable, the kind of guy everyone wants to know. But I also knew better than to mess with him, a good decision in light of his later achievements as a United States Marine.

Since I admired him so much, I felt a lot of dissonance when he decided to become a pastor after his military duties ended. I was an adolescent rebel determined to reject my parents' faith. I could rationalize my choice easily because they were just parents. What could they know? But Dave? He wasn't supposed to follow in their footsteps. He was too cool and tough to be a Christian.

Looking back, I am not sure how Dave's faith fit into my own choices, but I know it was one key to keeping me from falling away entirely. Seeing a guy up close who was smart enough to avoid getting duped made me give Christ a more serious look than I might have otherwise.

People like Dave sow mentoring seeds in children like parents can't. A student ministry leader once said it this way to me: "A child will respond to the oldest person in their world who will take them seriously." I've seen it. Children will look to other adults who will be friends to them.

Grandparents can make their presence felt in a big way. I was recently at the twenty-third birthday party for one of my friends' sons. Their family tradition is to read from the Bible before dinner, so as birthday boy he got to pick the passage. Before reading, he described the difficult week he'd had, but how the hardship had been eased by words written on a birthday card from his grandmother.

As they caught each other's eyes across the circle of family and friends, he looked into his Bible and read Christ's words, echoed two thousand years later from "Gram" to her grandson, "Come to me, all you who are weary and burdened, and I will give you rest."[22] Her nonstop spiritual influence was injected again. She is a grandmother who can touch a young man's soul like few others can and keep him walking with Christ.

Aunts and uncles can play the same role. I've seen it with Scott and Laurie Pederson, friends of ours from Willow Creek. Although they don't have children of their own, they are wonderful partners to their siblings and cousins . . . and their kids. Laurie once told me why. She had a favorite aunt who played a big role in her life and decisions, so she wanted to pass the legacy on to a third generation.

They aren't stuffy about it. Scott and Laurie are famous for their outrageous adventures, leading older cousins' outings to audacious locations, and taking toddler and elementary school nieces and nephews into fantasy worlds rivaling their favorite fairy tales. Years of fun and adventure make them naturals when the next generation needs adults other than their parents to talk to. They are a surrogate influence affecting dozens in their extended family to say yes to God again and again. They have intercepted behavior before it became delinquent, intervened when bad choices were about to be made, and injected powerful examples rooted in lasting relationship.

Maybe you don't have the influence of grandparents and uncles and aunts. Don't give up on the idea of partnering with others. My wife and I are constantly on the lookout for guys who can influence our sons. Sometimes the influence has been subtle, as with the casual conversations the boys and Jim Pluymert, my law partner, have had over baseball. Other times the influence has been direct, as in poignant interactions with someone of the stature of Bill Hybels.

Partnering with others may happen in random moments, because all it takes is adults who "get it." Phil was seven years old when we attended our first small group conference at Willow Creek. He was not exactly part of the target audience for the event, but I was fresh out of babysitters. So I prepped him to be on his best behavior—with a combination of threats and bribes—and off we went to the first session.

We snuck in as things started, only to find few places to sit. I sheepishly opted for two open seats next to Gilbert Bilezikian, the college professor who inspired the original vision for Willow Creek. I was intimidated by the idea of sitting with the distinguished founding elder. I didn't know whether to apologize or simply go back home.

Before I could decide, Gil welcomed Phil to his table, and there was no way he was letting his new little friend go. As it turned out, the hardest part of the experience was not making Phil behave, but Gil. He had more impact on Phil in that day than he can know. To this day, almost every time Dr. B and I cross paths, his first question is about how his little friend is doing. I don't have the heart to tell him his "little" friend is a foot taller than him. I tell him often, though, how Phil talks about Gil's welcome whenever Dr. B's name is mentioned.

Frank and Janice Yarosh are two of our best partners. It started when our kids were young, when they invited them over to their house for a night of good eating, followed by rollerblading in their basement, and going three on one in a basketball game against a shortened version of Frank playing from his knees to even the playing field.

Just last week, Frank was back. But this time it was not just to play in the basement. He let Mark drive his brand-new pickup truck. They ate some crummy burgers and went bowling, but none of that was the point. Mark and Tim were walking on air for several days because Frank spent time with them, took them seriously, and wanted to find out where their lives are going.

Sandi Seel was another gift to our family for a season. Due to travel demands tied to ministry at that time, we faced periodic needs for help. My parents lived locally and helped when they could, but three energetic guys drained them fast. Sandi was single and would move in for a few days at a time, but she wasn't just a babysitter. She dove in, sometimes literally headfirst, to dig into the lives of our boys. Although she now lives in California, she writes to them periodically to let them know she prays for them regularly and to encourage them to remain faithful to their upbringing.

The list goes on. Bill, Tim and Martha, Jim, John, Tim, Charlie and Diane, Wayne, Josh, Steve and Cindy, Eddie, Dave, Kevin, Troy, Scott, Brandon, Bobby, and many others have shared the parenting journey with us. Each of them owns a part of our kids' spiritual portfolio with us.

It has made us appreciate how we can influence other kids. We used those cues in our home decorating, creating a "kid room" to be a magnet for friends to hang out at our place. In the midst of the noise and food runs to the kitchen, we inevitably connect with them. Lynn's sewing room has given her the chance to be a partner to other moms and girls. She is amazing to watch with females of all ages through her passion for art, quilting, and other crafts. The conversations inevitably turn spiritual, because the activity provides a context for Lynn's spiritual gifts of shepherding and encouragement to ooze out. A similar experience with guys has helped me rationalize having a couple of fast motorcycles in the garage—you can use the enhanced credibility you will gain with your children's friends as an excuse for all kinds of toys. You *need* that boat, Jet Ski, snowmobile, hot rod, or sports car for the sake of your kids!

Our kids will reach adulthood accompanied by a nonstop flow of what can seem to be an oxymoron to adolescents: very cool Christians. They reinforce our tradition of Christian faith. But they each have a unique angle on how they made the choice to follow Christ, and have made it fun for our boys to see how others' choices attract them to our spiritual longing for them—to love and follow Christ.

Partnering with the Church

It always seems to be news to parents to hear their children cannot drive, so they are the ones who must bring them to church! The church is one of the best partners you have available to you.

The obvious starting point: your children's ministries. Most churches I know of are doing their level best to offer kids a great experience for an hour or two every week, or if they are not, they know it tops the list in strategic needs for their congregation. Help is readily available to reinforce the spiritual choices you hope your son or daughter will make. Add to that the great curricula, strategic thinking, and leadership training available these days, and you can't afford to settle for failing to connect with kids, leaving them bored with God.

Student ministries matter more than ever. In a world dominated by MTV, films, and music, the battlefront for our kids' souls has shifted from high school to the earliest stages of middle school. Why would you choose to forego the help available to you and your children? Having cut my ministry leadership teeth with junior high and high school students during a low-tech era, I recognize that these are remarkable days in the world of working with them.

That doesn't mean programs have to be all sizzle. Relationships matter more than ever. When we shifted our small group emphasis at Willow Creek, we decided to start small groups at age three. A great proportion of this generation's church kids, ours included, have grown up with small groups being normal. Each of my children can tell you the small group path they have walked, and the names of leaders who have kept them on the spiritual tightrope.

Both small group and ministry leaders have wisely included compassion efforts in the small group diet, so students can escape their suburban environment and mind-set. Over time, we have learned not to neglect the changes that can come from one mission trip or other experience like it. It may open up an opportunity for you to do something of spiritual impact with them, where you could be on the scene when they choose their spiritual future.

Partnership makes all the difference when facing the spiritual challenge. You need your children as your partners and can engage them most by understanding their spiritual pathway. Partner with each other with the same attention to your own unique styles. Watch for others who will team up with you along the way, and lean into every bit of help your church can provide.

What If I Came Late to the Party?

Before we leave this topic, let me add a quick word to those of you who are parents who discovered a personal relationship with God later in life, when your kids were older. Do not give up on how you might yet influence even grown children in this arena.

Your kids are watching you closer than you think, and sometimes the decision to attend to your spiritual side can have a profound impact on your children. As I heard Dr. Joseph Stowell teach years ago, "It takes a changing life to change a life." Your life change could ripple far.

For my friends who have come to Christ later in life, their ability to help their children in their spiritual journey correlates quite directly to their own authentic growth and life change. If you continue to grow and change in ways that seem appealing to your children, becoming more loving, more joyful, more peaceful, more patient, more kind, and so on, they will be affected more than you can imagine.

The spiritual tightrope never ends for any of us. This side of heaven, we all make fresh choices every day with eternal impact. Our kids face their own forks in the road at every turn, and the path they choose will be marked with the signposts we, and those we partner with, set before them. The journey will feel long and arduous at times, perilous and uncertain at others. The lows will be disheartening, the highs exhilarating. It all adds to the tension we live with all along the way. It puts the next tightrope in perspective, where we will continue to get accustomed to another balancing act parenting requires.

5

Are You Sure You Want to Die on That Hill?

The Adolescent Challenge

Selective ignorance, a cornerstone of child rearing. You don't put kids under surveillance: it might frighten you. Parents should sit tall in the saddle and look upon their troops with a noble and benevolent and extremely nearsighted gaze.[1]

Garrison Keillor

If I thought parenting was a challenge when my kids were little, it was nothing compared to the first days of preadolescence. The shift came suddenly.

A few years ago, I came home from work to two things. The first was Lynn, standing at the door with the fiercest look of anger I'd ever seen. The second: an aroma I had first smelled on my high school bus decades earlier. Lynn quickly named it when she exclaimed, "I just caught Mark smoking marijuana in his room!" She was steamed, and Mark was in hiding, in fear for his life.

We eventually heard the whole story. One of Mark's friends had given him a marijuana joint. He claimed not to know what it was for sure. He really didn't know how to smoke the thing. His friend was a real Einstein too; he told Mark to use his room as his hideaway smoking lounge because it had hardwood floors, so there was no carpet to soak up the smell. Since neither of them had any sense of the unique odor marijuana emits, they never anticipated the trap they were walking into. And Mark never inhaled, meaning he can still be president.

Fortunately for him, he was repentant, spilled the whole story, and took his discipline without complaint. Fortunately for us, we can now look back at it and laugh, especially because that bad behavior was momentary. In fact, Mark has told the story to many friends and permitted me to write about his short-lived venture into narcotics.

Up to that day I thought a dozen years of parenting would make me better at it. But then adolescence hit, and any such illusions were quickly shattered. Despite my wishful thinking that being a dad would get easier over time, the intensity of parenting increased rapidly. The risks associated with bad behavior raise the stakes more than ever. Now that Phil, Mark, and Tim are eighteen, sixteen, and fourteen, it feels like I might be going backward in child-rearing effectiveness.

In some ways the load is lighter; there is nothing like enduring sleep deprivation, smelly diapers, and chronic wailing during children's infancy, or the constant watchfulness and unending correction toddlers require. Those eras leave you exhausted.

But what you learn then provides little preparation for what awaits when infants and toddlers turn into bundles of adolescent confusion. No matter what your experience has been up to that point, the outcome of your early investment in your kids is far from certain. You find out all over again how parenting really is life's biggest challenge.

102

Coping with All That Uncertainty

A few days ago, I ate lunch with a couple I am just getting to know. They enjoy a terrific reputation in their community, work, ministry, and family. I knew little about their children, so I asked about them. I poked past the initial, "safe" information, and then their story took a turn.

Through the middle and high school years their oldest, a daughter, had been the model child. She had it all—a heart for God, smarts in school, achievements galore, church involvement, leadership to peers, good looks, exemplary behavior, and a bright future filled with apparent success. Mom and dad were seen as child-rearing whizzes, those who had gotten it "right."

But then, during her senior year, their sweet little girl not only digressed from her picture-perfect future, she completely derailed almost every part of her life. Within weeks she had dropped out of her activities, picked up drinking and drugs, and pushed against every form of engagement. Her parents were blindsided but moved quickly to find as many constructive responses as they could.

This is not an uncommon story. It does not always end happily. For this family today, almost one year later, their daughter has responded well to a dramatic family intervention and is completing the late stages of a recovery program. But she is an uncertain distance from resolving years of hidden confusion and anger.

When I asked this wounded but wiser mom and dad how they coped with the shocking turn, I liked their starting point. "The first thing we had to do," they confessed, "was to fall on our knees and repent of all our harsh judgments of parents who experienced what we did. We thought we had the best kid because of our parenting skill. All the things we said about others . . . we got humbled real fast." It is so easy to slip into the "that could never happen to us" mode, isn't it?

103

They went on to describe the daily battle they now face when showing their daughter love. Love was easy when she had been so good. They still held the same unqualified affection they did when she toed their line, but the way they show it now demands constant regulation. Sometimes their daughter needs *tender love*, and sometimes she needs *tough love*. Love has to be applied with care to the complexities their family is living through, including their ongoing bewilderment about a vague future.

I know plenty of families whose stories are not as happy as this one. An otherwise wholesome daughter shows up pregnant; a supposedly compliant son is the subject of a call from the police; a family's illusion of nonstop warmth and fondness is shattered by bad choices. Loving your kids is simple when all is well. As they turn over a behavioral apple cart or two when they're older, suddenly it is not so effortless. Twist the path into outright adolescent rebellion, shattering all you thought you knew about how to raise kids the "right" way, and you will be struggling to regain your balance.

Tightropes and Teenagers

Let's assume the first decade of parenting goes fine, and you are well on your way to helping your kids through the first phase of growing up. Be aware that no matter how things go for the first dozen years or so, adolescence is coming. Your chances of being humbled increase exponentially. The severity of consequences is sky high. The likelihood of being knocked clean off the parenting tightrope may be just around the bend. It is tough to stay upright and steady between what may prove to be the most difficult polarities to keep in tension, *the adolescent challenge*:

Tender Love ——————————————— Tough Love

On one end of the continuum, when children take the turn to adolescent independence, they need the assurance of as much tender love as they can find. Knowing it, feeling it, and experiencing it is all part of what steadies them when they are most prone to lose their way.

But then, without losing an ounce of the need for absolute affection, a son or daughter in outright rebellion needs tough love. Although tender love and tough love will feel like they battle each other, once again the answer will be yes to both, together.

In some ways, the adolescent challenge picks up a theme from the last chapter: the story of the prodigal son, one of the best pictures of unconditional acceptance. In Jesus's story, despite this rebellious son running off and squandering some of his dad's wealth, the dad waits and watches. When the son returns, he rushes out to meet him and receives him back without condition.

Jesus described how that mirrors God and the unconditional acceptance awaiting each of us. God really will accept you, no matter what you've done. Moreover, he wants us to give each other that same kind of love. He wants parents to give that kind of love to their kids. Why? God is convinced love will inevitably win the day.

Does that mean God is a doormat? No. God walks the tough love tightrope too. He says so in Hebrews 12:5–6: "My son, do not make light of the Lord's discipline, and do not lose heart when he rebukes you, because the Lord disciplines those he loves, and he punishes everyone he accepts as a son." From time to time, even if you give your life to him, God will impose behavioral limits. He unconditionally accepts us, but occasionally he puts tough love into play, most often when we engage in a pattern of playing outside the lines.

We parents face the same challenge. How do you get through the adolescent era with minimal damage? Realize you will live in the tension between tough and tender love.

You find some of the flavor of doing both in Galatians 6:1: "if someone is caught in a sin, you who are spiritual should restore him gently." While this instruction applies to the more general context of the church and how we should hold each other accountable in redemptive ways, I think it is a good principle for parents to apply when it comes time to walk the tightrope strung between tender love and tough love.

On the "tough love" side, be on the lookout for sin. Don't ignore it. Expect it. Face it. You will have to be hard-hitting, call it what it is, and deal with it. When your kids rebel, your response matters.

But all of that—what will feel harsh and unbending at times—has to be imposed with a mind-set of restorative intervention. The "gentle" or "tender love" side of engaging with a wrong-headed adolescent will demand delicate engagement. If it feels nearly impossible, you are living right where an acrobat finds their greatest high-wire challenge.

Making restorative intervention happen isn't easy. But we have observed five ways that have kept us on the adolescent tightrope, restoring wayward rebels gently.

1. Be Hands-Off

The first and greatest temptation most parents feel is to rescue their teenagers when they make bad choices. The call comes from school about something your son has done. The neighbor stops by to tell you about what they saw your daughter doing in the neighborhood. The police contact you about adolescent mischief that went too far.

We want to respond the same as when they got in trouble as little kids. You are naturally inclined to protect them if you can. You still love your son, for example, like you did when he fell off his bike. You want to make the pain go away.

Our thinking was challenged by Jeff VanVonderen's book, *Families Where Grace Is in Place.*[2] It is one of the best books we have found on meeting the parenting challenge generally, and the adolescent challenge specifically. VanVonderen prescribes a fundamental parenting practice: allow natural consequences to inflict the pain needed to produce changed behavior.

When we first read it, that thought made sense. But when we reviewed our history and started to monitor our own behavior as a real live mom and dad, the frequency with which we were unwilling to allow our boys to live with the consequences of their behavior shocked us. And we had the reputation (not only by our kids' reckoning) of being pretty strict!

The routine for us, and for most parents we compared notes with, was to rescue children from pain. It was a good knee-jerk reaction sometimes, because we wanted to be sure our children knew the boundless love we had for them. While that might be an appropriate reaction with toddlers, it can be dead wrong with teens. As they become increasingly capable of making their own choices—good ones that produce positive fruit and bad ones that will leave a sour taste—we have to change.

Are there times you should rescue your kids? Sure. Should you occasionally allow them to wallow in some hard circumstances of their own doing? You bet. At some point you will have to censor your inclination toward tender love. You will have to move down the tightrope toward the kind of tough love that allows a willful son or defiant daughter to experience the consequences of their own decisions, unadulterated by your involvement, in the hope that short-term cost will prevent long-term wounds. Maintaining your balance will force you into hard decisions more often than you want.

There are numerous situations, some less hurtful than others, when being hands-off might be just the right response.

- *Work:* There will be more on this issue in the next chapter, but tough love allows natural consequences to hit kids with a marginal work ethic. At some point in adolescents' development, they need to know the consequence of no work—no money. As harsh as it might sound, even the

Bible says it, "If a man will not work, he shall not eat."[3] I have yet to see my sons starve, but they have missed opportunities for fun adventure, desirable stuff, and social events because from time to time they are required to cover the cost of part of their existence. Whether through a squandered allowance or taking a pass on available work, unmet desire for cash has left them sad about life, angry at us. External voices (especially theirs, but maybe the voices of other parents who see it differently too) and internal inklings will make you think you are not showing love to your children. You are, just the tough kind.

- *Jobs:* Once teenagers get jobs of their own, their work ethic gets tested by someone other than mom or dad. Parents know the real consequences that await a daughter with a cavalier attitude about her job performance or a son who is irresponsible with work. Unconditional affection presses some parents to take far too much responsibility for finding their kids a job, trying to intervene to make sure they perform well, or even overlooking poor performance when they work in a parent's business. One of the best experiences for some adolescents is to get fired. Even if there is a hint of injustice in it, losing a job as a natural consequence for less than optimal performance is terrific preparation for later life.

- *Schedules:* Do you have any trouble getting your teenagers out of bed? Most kids make notoriously bad choices about getting to sleep, so getting up on time is not even in the cards. We felt considerable irritation over chronic wake-up calls we felt obligated to render but did little to change anything for a long time. We felt doomed to provide taxi service for the extra morning rides to school. The umpteenth argument over blowing past alarms, snooze buttons, and "reminders" delivered at varied intensity finally woke us up. We needed the pain of consequences to take over. So we made a deal. We would wake each guy up one or two times, but after that they were on their own. If they missed their ride or bus, too bad. They could call a cab, or pay us the cab fare for the needed service. Our schools rub salt in the tardiness wounds via detention too. Our kids still blow it, but pain has cured a lot of bad choices. It is painful for us to watch, but far less than the alternative.

- *Planning:* We've heard it as often as you have. "I'm so bored." Lynn is inclined to overreact to those plaintive and pitiful whines by cranking up a treadmill of suggestions, ideas, and opportunities awaiting someone who will take the initiative. None of it usually works, either because most of her remedies for boredom required them to plan hours or days before or to take some immediate initiative. They won't do either. I like the response one friend has to gripes about life turned dull. "What a sad state to find yourself in," she will respond, with just a hint of sarcasm. "With all the things in our world to do, to end up bored is about as pitiful as it gets." Tough love gets put into action by her refusal to fix the problem. That has worked better for us as well. No initiative, no rescue from boredom. Bad planning, missed chances. A passive attitude produces pain enough to make a change next time.

- *Grades:* So far we have been blessed with children who, though they periodically struggle with school, have the combination of academic ability and diligence to do good work and be likely college candidates. Other parents we've walked with have struggled on this tightrope due to borderline grades. Clearly, love demands we get to the bottom of learning disabilities and other issues affecting schoolwork, and we all have to impose a certain level of discipline to build sound study habits and the like. But the need for tough love has pressed some great

109

parents to allow natural consequences to impact their underachieving son or daughter. The experience has been painful, because it has meant some time at summer school for flunked classes, staying a grade behind, temporary dropouts, and deferred college. Other parents seem to be in well-meaning denial over the roots of academic failure, and badger, manipulate, or otherwise attempt to force their students into an educational future destined for defeat due to the choices students have to make in the end. A dose of tough love may be needed.

- *Friends:* Let's face it. Some children are socially awkward. It may be over things they can't control, such as a handicap, prejudice, or family circumstances. But sometimes they face a kind of relational unawareness their parents are unwilling to correct. By the time they are teens, their patterns of abusing friendship or social ineptitude get them in hot water. Mom and dad either sit on the sidelines mutely allowing it without comment or instruction or try to save a child from the impact of their inappropriate interaction with people. I say this without any desire to be unsympathetic, but relying on points of pain may actually be opening an opportunity for their son or daughter to learn some things about social adjustment, albeit through what could be momentary rejection. Tender love is the appropriate inner response, but you might need to allow tough-love consequences to help a child learn social skills that can only come from interacting with their world. This also gives you the opportunity to explain relational reality.

- *Mistakes:* Carelessness is one of the toughest parts of life we all learn to deal with. Most of the time, we make mistakes that cost us little. Once in a while, though, there is a doozy, such as our first car wreck, a lost wallet or other item of value, or missed deadlines through simple oversight. Our own sense of relief when our mistakes

110

are met with mercy can motivate us to cover kids' gaffes with grace. Sometimes that is OK. Other times? You may want to meet your son or daughter's plea for a rescue from their carelessness because "it wasn't my fault" with a dose of reality. Once in a while, we have to live with the consequences of our mistakes. It's a part of life. Parents who too often intercept the results of such lapses develop children who don't connect what they do or fail to do with the outcomes they will face for a lifetime later.

- *Transportation:* One inescapable part of adolescence is the terrifying prospect of a sixteen- or seventeen-year-old getting a license to drive. It feels like we're handing them a loaded gun. And yet many kids think driving is a right, not a privilege, a right that comes complete with coverage from mom and dad for the expense of car ownership. Expenses that include paying for lawyers to get kids off the hook for tickets, even providing substitute transportation upon loss of license. Sometimes the rationale seems good for families who have the resources to provide it. But that is little preparation for reality. Is there a right answer in all this? No. It is part of parenting on a tightrope. But should you be aware of the tension between the tender love that may push you away from allowing tough love consequences to have their way when it comes to this rite of passage to driving? Maybe. Loss of license could mean your child ends up riding the bus, walking, or riding a bike. Will that be embarrassing to them? Yep. And perhaps a great teacher.

- *Arrests:* Lynn and I were enjoying coffee and dessert with friends one evening while our church youth group was on an outing. A loud knock on the door interrupted our conversation. Standing on the step was a police officer with Mark, then thirteen, in tow. He and other students had been placing junk on local railroad tracks, and they caught Mark while others got away.

111

Since he wouldn't squeal on his friends, they wanted us to lean on him to spill the beans. Mark remained stone silent. The officer decided to leave Mark in our custody, rejoining other law enforcement officers in trying to catch the other kids. We consoled Mark while recovering from our own distress. Then another knock on the door. I angrily answered it . . . and a "candid camera" caught my reaction to our student's prank. The whole situation was made up! Although I was relieved in the moment, later reflection showed me how much tension there would have been if this had been real. If one of your kids is caught in illegal activity, what do you do? I've seen some parents spare no expense or effort saving their obviously guilty son or daughter from time in jail. More than once I discerned it was an ill-advised rescue, and the better course would be to allow a courtroom to teach lessons some will learn no other way. There is no right answer but that the tension must be faced.

- *Authority:* Parents who will bail their kids out of legal hot water may face a corresponding dilemma at school. Trouble with school authorities may produce suspension or expulsion, or getting kicked off of athletic teams, artistic troupes, or academic groups. You have to pick your spots for mercy—occasionally and wisely letting them or getting them off the hook is good—but do not allow your rightful, undying compassion for your own child to cloud your objectivity. Stay on the tightrope and candidly assess whether you need to walk toward a tougher stance, one that may align you with other authorities who may not be perfect, but who are on to something about your son or daughter that must be addressed for their own, ultimate good. Resilient adolescents who are developing healthy character will rebound from hard lines of authority even if they disagree.

112

- *Girlfriends:* Not to be sexist or a biased dad of only sons, but boys need training on how to treat girls well. Tough love can be a great way to do the teaching. Taking a cue from other effective parents, I require my boys to have a conversation with the girl's parents over date details before plans are finalized, and a "debrief session" with a girl's dad when curfew got blown or itineraries were creatively reshaped to include activity parents never would have approved. Nothing like a guy having to face a gal's dad—or her older brothers—to shape his future choices. This can be part of the tough love equation, and the stories that spread will provide plenty of incentive to be on their best behavior and do whatever they can to dodge having to confront a girl's angry mother or father.

These are just a few examples of tough love situations. The point is not to prescribe or imply "right" answers, but rather to help each of us anticipate where we're disinclined to allow consequences to teach needed lessons. Reflect on your own patterns, and then monitor your reactions in the days ahead. How often is your first response to rescue?

2. Be Explicit

Not everything an adolescent needs to learn has a natural consequence. Uncompleted household chores only leave the mess. Undisciplined time only creates frustration. Unrelenting challenges to your authority only produce yelling, discord, and repeat performances.

Some attitudes demand more focus or attention than natural consequences provide. You know your son or daughter's tendencies and deficits best and whether they are "getting it." If they are not, added consequences may be called for.

113

The problem: you may have to create consequences. How do I know? This is nothing short of a constant rub with Lynn. She admits it. She gets so frustrated with Phil, Mark, and Tim over their choices and mistakes that she is more affected than they are. They run in with last minute news of a field trip they forgot, so in the next nanosecond they must have a signed permission, a check for a zillion dollars, and a ride to Detroit. They overlook a deadline for a church retreat, but Lynn is supposed to lobby the entire universe for a pardon. They make plans with friends but overlook critical details on schedule, travel, and size of bus needed to get all forty-three of them to the destination, and suddenly it is her problem to solve.

Harder still are other, more tense moments. They take teasing too far and hurt her feelings. They slight her when new friends come to our home, revealing their poorly hidden opinion she is not quite cool enough to introduce. They resist her authority by responding only if Dad says it, ridiculing her ability to enforce her tough stance on an issue, or showing outright defiance against her requests or requirements.

Lynn, being naturally loving, does her fair share of swallowing hard, swinging into action, making stuff happen, realizing kids will be kids, and living with some of the calluses good parents must form. But over time, an embittered spirit can take root. She would like them to learn to take more responsibility, be more considerate of others affected by their actions, and show care for their mom.

Her wish? That they would just do the right thing, like she would. The problem is that a teenage boy does not think like a mature adult. Lynn realizes that but knows it requires hard work that she hates to do: if she wants them to change, she needs to take the responsibility to create consequences for behavior where there are no natural ones.

While Lynn bears the brunt of these dynamics due to being on the scene more often when the daily crises happen, we have learned the hard way to help each other create consequences. We can both get caught by our wish for adolescents to act like fortysomethings. Our conversations go something like this:

Parent #1: "You won't believe what [insert son's name here] did."

Parent #2: "Try me."

Parent #1: "[insert latest catastrophe here]."

Parent #2: "Yeah?"

Parent #1: "I can't believe they would do that!"

Parent #2: "What planet are you from?" (A polite way to say "shut up.")

Parent #1: "Oh."

Parent #2: "What do you want them to do instead?"

Parent #1: "[insert expectation here]."

Parent #2: "Did you tell them ahead of time?"

Parent #1: "No."

Parent #2: "Did you warn them what would happen if they didn't?"

Parent #1: "Noooooo!" (said with a tone of regret for beginning the conversation)

Parent #2: "You remember the definition of insanity?"

Parent #1: "Yes."

Both of us, in unison: "Doing the same thing over again, but expecting a different result."

I retell this conversation not to depict either of us as wiser than the other. In fact, the reason we have this exchange as often as we do is because we can both lose the plot. It requires a measure of toughness to be willing to create consequences for conduct.

Here is what we've learned we have to do if there are no natural consequences:

115

Key #1: *Clearly* state the expected behavior.

Key #2: *Clearly* state a warning for failure (the consequence you define).

Key #3: *Clearly* cite expectations and warnings when imposing the consequence.

For example, one of our sons got on a roll of challenging our authority, demonstrating a chronic bad attitude, and being generally disagreeable whenever he could. We tried lots of remedies, including letting him suffer with the outcomes of his bad choices. Nothing changed the situation from going from bad to worse. He was turning into nothing short of a resident jerk, with no change in sight. Given no correction, this was going to end up being a trend line to losing him.

After some background work, I finally sat him down and explained our concern, which he knew quite well from all the contention in our household. I gave numerous specific examples of the attitudes and actions needing change and described what we wanted instead (Key #1). If he did not change, I told him, he would need to process his issues with Sergeant Carter at a military academy, for which I had the brochures if he would like to review them (Key #2). He had one week to give me his decision.

When we talked again seven days later, he opted to remain a resident of our home. No surprise. The alternative wasn't too attractive. But a month later, when the same old demons plagued him all over again, I told him why he should begin packing his bags (Key #3). Due to the drastic nature of the consequence, I gave him a three-day reprieve so he could take another look at the brochures. He decided he wouldn't engage in further behavior that would get him a change of address.

There are many, far less dramatic examples. We have charged our kids for services when they wouldn't do their chores or clean their rooms; we figured if one of us had to do it, we should pick up their allowance (which makes us much more cheerful about taking up the slack). If you have a son or daughter who hates losing money, this can be a good way to wake them up to what they need to stay on top of.

Imposing schedules on the guys has helped them when they most wanted to hang loose but needed structure. We let them know our expectations for managing a day's activity, let them know how we would run things for them if they didn't, and when they chose to remain on their non-schedule, we imposed ours for a week or two.

I know of one family who responded to recurrent bad choices regarding friends by creating consequences for their teenage daughter. Mom and dad made clear the poor relational choices she was making and gave her time to navigate the difficult transition she needed to begin. They also made clear they would switch the school she was attending if she did not take action. This was a hard one; she didn't think they would do it. They did. She went to the new high school kicking and screaming, threatening to run away. But then she started making the friendship transitions she needed to make. It was chaotic, but her folks' willingness to get tough made the difference.

One benefit of giving kids the keys to a car is the ability to take them back. Doing so without warning seems harsh for the kid who most treasures freedom, but if you define expected behavior, warn them keys hang in the balance, and then take custody when they blow it, their behavior may change quicker.

There is no magic to this and no guaranteed outcomes, either. It is about constructing penalties that will affect behavioral choices. If their options carry no price, they are free to choose anything. Figuring out what they most value and attaching the consequence to that can be one of the best gifts you can give them. And it will make you less arbitrary and capricious in how you parent them, especially through the adolescent years.

3. Be Flexible

"Be flexible" sounds like a contradiction to "be explicit," right? In some ways it is. We're not drawing dot-to-dot. We're walking a tightrope, and you may need to regain your balance through different means, especially if you naturally tend toward the tough love end of the continuum too often, or if natural or created consequences aren't doing the trick.

A couple of good counselors taught us to ask the question, "What do you really want?" early and often. Not just of our kids. Of ourselves too. We needed to learn not only when to negotiate with our sons, but also to teach them how to negotiate for what they want. It has turned us from some unthinking, unduly hard-lined responses once in a while.

Think about it. Kids tend to get more demanding in adolescence. And we tend to get more inflexible with age. Negotiation, at the appropriate time over the right issues, can help both you and your teenagers.

One of our never-ending debates seems to be over curfews. Phil is in his senior year of high school as I write, soon to be an adult and out of our house in college. Recently, he started to chafe at our midnight curfew. Tempted to be tough on our stance, at first I refused to even discuss any change. It was midnight for me, so it would stay midnight for him. To his credit, Phil asked if we could discuss it further. When we did, he was prepared to engage constructively. He told me how his friends all had 1:00 a.m. curfews, so it was embarrassing for him to leave early and crimped their ability to make plans sometimes. I made him a deal. He could stay out until 1:00 if he got out of bed the next morning when it was time for work and family activities, in any event no later than noon. He wasn't wild about that prospect until I reassured him I wouldn't be goofy about making up reasons for early wake-up calls. So he agreed. I agreed too, but only after verifying with a couple of other parents who had backed down their curfew to 1:00—I am unconditional in my love, but tough on trust in such negotiations.

Other examples of negotiating flexibility include the following:

- If they will return one or more items in a collection of new clothing they overspent on, some of which is flatly unwise to keep, offer to reimburse them for part of what they retain. That's what some of our friends recently did. Rather than get mad at their daughter's spending habits, they created an incentive so she could learn what it feels like to make wiser buying assessments, while saving some of the cost she would bear otherwise.

- When they start driving, have them pay for their own insurance. If they complain about the cost, let them decide whether to add collision coverage, and receive a financial benefit (and the corresponding risk) for taking a pass on it. We did that with Phil. When he opted to save the monthly insurance cost, he had to dig into his pocket to repair a later fender bender. That cost was less than the collision insurance, so he is ahead . . . for now. He also drives more carefully.

- As they choose between school, church, or volunteer activities which may mean they cannot work and earn spending money they would like to have, vary the funds you provide in exchange for them continuing a non-paying activity you deem good for them. One dad we know varies allowances based on his kids' level of extra-curricular and charitable involvement. He figures they'll learn all about work in due course, and values the exercise of their volunteer muscles in the meantime.

- Rather than simply providing some or all of the purchase price for something they would like to have, suggest they sell something of value in exchange. Our kids play lots of instruments, and always have their eye on the next guitar,

119

drum, or sound gear. Rather than simply accumulate more, we've encouraged them to be more creative. If they liquidate some of their old gear, we provide a little more help with the next purchase.

- Reward preferred choices. We have friends who provide a newer car to a child who letters in two sports, a lesser quality one for one sport, and a "beater" if no sports are pursued.
- Put limits on college tuition help, and negotiate the means to obtaining the maximum level of your aid. You can match scholarships they get or funds they save rather than simply fund all education as a matter of right. This way the young man or woman is engaged in the process of funding his or her own higher education.

The point here is not about finding right and wrong answers. You may disagree with what you see other parents do. The point is about finding a way to middle ground when staying too tough may disserve you and one of your kids. It will help them learn about their own preferences and acquire a skill they will need later in life.

4. Be Constructive

I started my legal career as a trial lawyer, working a mix of court cases, from defending engineers and architects for malpractice claims to pursuing banks' claims to recover on unpaid loans and bankruptcy losses, from divorce and custody matters to criminal defense work. One thing the criminal cases taught me was to see them as two cases, really. The first is over a defendant's guilt or innocence. The second involves their sentence for what they did wrong. It is not uncommon for a person to know they will be convicted, so a lawyer's focus is negotiating or contesting the sentence a prosecutor wants to impose.

There is considerable philosophical debate over what criminal sentencing is supposed to do, whether it is to merely punish or to rehabilitate. I think both are needed. Wrongdoing deserves a certain degree of retribution to be a disincentive to repeat behavior. However, if punishment can rehabilitate as well, then so much the better.

Parents are to some extent like judges at sentencing. You punish, and you rehabilitate if you can. The sentencing process provides a frame of reference for how to make tough love as constructive as it can be. It will still have the raw edge of needed punishment. But if you use it with the motivation, born of your tender love, to rehab that which drives bad behavior, you may find the adolescent challenge easier to survive.

Wise judges and discerning parents both start out considering whether there may be a medical or psychological condition driving the behavior they must punish and change, and how that should affect any future limits. That makes particular sense with kids. Doctors, psychologists, and social workers have been heroic for many families in need of wisdom to determine whether their daughter is misbehaving because of a chemical imbalance, or their son's rebellion is rooted in early life trauma or tangled thinking patterns. It takes tough love to get them in front of the right professionals to figure that out, but it saves kids from lifelong dysfunction, and it saves dad or mom from trying to correct something that demands more than mere punishment.

"Probation" or a "suspended sentence" may be a right approach in some situations. Once you hear the evidence and find them guilty, impose the penalty . . . but then tell your child you will suspend it if they toe the line, but will fully impose the sentence if they violate the terms of probation. Require restitution if there has been damage or other costs. Set explicit conditions for good behavior. This allows them to feel some measure of tough love with both punishment and the chance to change. You may find it more constructive to go for what we as parents are ultimately after—real change—rather than hitting them with the full weight of what they otherwise deserve.

We have run the equivalent of a "work release program," where they are grounded for everything but specified activities we deem helpful to attitude or conduct. They lose the birthday party but are allowed to attend youth group. They are confined to their room but can get out when it is spic and span. They can reduce the time they have to serve by getting specified jobs done well. From time to time the work has been unattractive enough for them to opt to serve out their imprisonment, at least at first. If an attractive opportunity comes their way, though, then they change course after counting the cost of their poor choice. A good outcome if your objective is learning.

On other occasions, both conduct and character are so bad that we've gone to the other extreme. Solitary confinement, or "being in lockdown," as we call it, can be strong but needed medicine to cure a deteriorating series of behaviors, and give lots of time for reflection. Don't be cruel with it; there are stories of parents who have taken this idea way too far. Denying food, putting kids in unsuitable rooms, and other abusive measures are beyond the pale. I would *never* advocate this approach. But appropriate stretches of isolation, imposed with measured wisdom, can be a useful means to intensify punishment already imposed if the original proves insufficient to achieve the goal of rehabilitation.

You also may want to consider the concept provided by what are known as "recidivist laws," where repeat convictions lead to increasing punishment. It allows you one response to a first instance of failure—"strike one"—a more intense response for strike two, and some more ultimate response to strike three. We've found it constructive to let our boys know we are going lighter on a strike one offense, with the implication that punishment for strike two will be considerably more unpleasant. If they insist on swinging and missing three times, at least we've allowed them the opportunity for a constructive response before hitting the punishment wall.

We have also stumbled into how productive it can be to use "community service" as a form of sentencing. One time we had gone well past strike three, and little had worked to rehab bad behavior. If for no other reason than to try something different, an idea occurred to me. The next time I "imposed sentence" we required one of our kids to participate in three upcoming community service projects at our church. After a night serving in a homeless shelter, a day helping tote a semi load of items donated to a clothing and household goods drive, and a weekend's work at a Habitat for Humanity construction site, we saw the change we had hoped for. Tough love unwittingly accomplished two ends: help to others and a little change of heart.

Some parents have had to go further, much further. Their son or daughter has acted out so severely that they have been left with little choice but to pursue an intervention program. You can find out about these through good juvenile counselors, but you should screen the intervener carefully to fit your teenager's situation and your spiritual bent. Some of them have been the safety net needed to rescue an adolescent and their parents when there seems to be no mix of tender and tough love that will keep them on the tightrope.

5. Be Collaborative

I've said it before. Parenting may be one of the loneliest activities you will do. It doesn't have to be. We didn't know that at first. It was probably our competitive nature, wanting to be the best parents around, or our pride, not wanting to be found out as so confused as we were. Once we got over ourselves, collaborating with other parents was one of the best things we have found to get through some of the tougher days of adolescence.

123

Our best collaborations started after one of our kids got caught, along with a group of their friends, doing something illegal. Fortunately for us, it wasn't the police who caught them, but we knew the situation demanded swift and serious confrontation. Since I was scratching my head on the best way to go at it, I decided to swallow my pride just enough to admit one of my kids was capable of such activity and find out how our friends handled their situation.

"Have you talked to the parents of the other kids involved," they asked. Duh. No. "What will come of that," I wondered out loud. "Well, you'll find out that if the kids know all the parents are aware, and you have all agreed this can't ever happen again, it will have a lot more impact. And if you gather all the families and kids in one room to talk about the incident, your unified front may get the job done."

We tried it. It worked! Since then, we have had several "adolescent/parent conferences" (one was big enough to be better termed a convention) in ours and others' homes. It can be a hard but effective forum for debriefing after parties gone wild, excessive drinking, lowered sexual standards, and other issues where parents need a singular voice in the face of unified peer influence gone awry. Use it as a forum for stories from or about teenagers who made a bad choice, only to pay the rest of their lives for it. There is nothing like a group of adolescents looking into the eyes of a group of parents who are bound and determined to let them know they are unconditionally loved by a community.

There may be no other time where they need parenting so much, but are so unlikely to get it. They won't go looking for it. As one friend has observed, "Kids will always seek the parental vacuum." It's true. A house with no parents is a dangerous Nirvana to adolescents.

So, one of our "community standards" is that, whenever the roving band of teenagers is hanging out at each others' homes, parents work together to be sure at least one parent is present.

124

It doesn't always work, but we've all found out how trouble tends to correlate to parental absence.

Whenever possible, we prefer it to be someone who has been part of our multifamily discussions over expected conduct. However, once you become used to collaborating with others, it is not hard to check in with newer parents to find out their stances on key issues. The parents all usually agree, despite our kids' assertions we are the only parents out of touch with the rest of the world.

We now collaborate well ahead of certain events, such as homecoming, prom, Halloween, New Year's Eve, and the like. Uniform curfews and advance plans, with the consent of a team of households, can turn our fears over what kids might do into enjoyable rites of passage and holidays.

Every time we discuss parenting standards with other, inner-circle parents, we come away wiser. We usually find out we have a lot more in common than we thought   sometimes others are stricter! And we are mutually encouraged to hang tough through the chaos of getting children through adolescence.

Taking the Long View

Getting past all the juvenile minefields with minimal damage will tax both your patience and strength. But that is the point. Getting past. Getting through. Getting to the other side, where our children will have accumulated enough mistakes, choices, correction, and rehabilitation to live their own lives as adults. Most of them make it through just fine by the time they leave high school. Some of them take a little longer, but get on with it soon enough. A few will take the long way around. A small handful of kids whose parents tried to get the best mix—tender love *and* tough love—reject it. Parents are left with broken hearts and confused thoughts.

The confused thoughts have little remedy. As much as we'd like easy answers to the adolescent challenge, there are few

125

simple ones. If we treat it as a tension between two good things, and stay on the tightrope, we'll have done our best, which is all we can do.

If you're left with a broken heart, it is the best indicator your love has staying power. Every time you feel the pain, take it as a prompt to pray and to stay hopeful there can still be a turnaround. Your prayers touch the heart of a heavenly Father with limitless love for you *and* your child, and who understands how free will can ruin what should be treasured. Once you can no longer influence your children's choices, your boundless affection is a good gift you can always give. It may have more redemptive power in the long run than you imagined.

6

Be All That You Can Be

The Financial Challenge

Adults are always asking little kids what they want to be when they grow up because they are looking for ideas.[1]

Paula Poundstone

Imagine a company operating for years with no financial statements, no monetary controls, no understanding of where it stands economically. It opens up two or three branch operations but imposes no accountability for spending and does not teach its branches any ability to operate profitably as their business unit matures. Instead, the main office simply feeds each branch doses of cash as they have need.

Headquarters has little choice, really, since it never gets around to infusing financial management expertise into each of the operations. The hope is that each business unit will somehow make enough to be able to sustain their functions. Nobody is really sure this approach is going to work, except that this management style has somehow succeeded for the main office.

It has no strategic plan for the future. It has no intent to get everyone in the company to focus on the practical financial side of running a viable business. Low-grade anxiety plagues everybody when they wake up to a new day of trying to make it in an increasingly complex, expensive, competitive economic environment.

Nobody in their right mind would ever run a company that way, right? And yet that is how many households operate in our society. Mom or dad, as manager of the family finances, has little grip on fiscal reality. Despite twenty years of opportunity to prepare a child for a "spin-off," they take relatively few measures to assure the independent operation will be able to stand on its own two feet, let alone succeed impressively on its own. Oh, they might fund college or a trade-school education, which gives their daughter or son a sense of eventual economic independence. But the nuts and bolts of creating a budget, allocating resources, and planning for the future is given little thought, even though our kids are going to have to survive in a more costly, rapidly changing, and cutthroat world.

Some of you might even be surprised to find *the financial challenge* in a list of six key parenting issues. Face it: the reason this matters so much is that, once kids leave your home, they are likely to devote over 25 percent of their waking hours to work, and how well they do vocationally will define much of their lifestyle, relational world, and economic future. Once they begin earning money, their financial management skills will determine where they go, what they do, and how they impact our world. The financial challenge calls for a far greater focus than many parents give it.

The Tightrope Avoidance Syndrome

Children will be way down the road of life before they are economically viable. *Support*, and lots of it, will be required for a long time. Even after they begin to work toward independence, they will need a safety net—financial backing from their parents—if they are to make it in this world.

However, at some point they need to be *self-sufficient*. You don't want to support them forever. In fact, you'd like them to get to a place where they can support you in the manner to which you've become accustomed!

My friend Lee Strobel faced this issue with his son, Kyle. Lee and I were in a small group together as Kyle toiled his way through high school, finally caught fire academically in college, and found his unique gifts and passion in the field of philosophy. When Kyle told Lee he was aiming at a doctorate in philosophy, Lee responded, "Do you know the difference between a philosopher and a pizza? A pizza can feed a family of four."

Kyle has completed most of his schooling now, and I don't know if he has figured out how he'll feed a family of four, but Lee used humor to place a truth in front of his son. He has to get to the place where he can be self-sufficient.

First Timothy 5:8 makes that truth about as raw as it gets: "But anyone who won't care for his own relatives when they need help, especially those living in his own family, has no right to say he is a Christian" (TLB).

How are our kids going to arrive at that destination? How do you move each of your kids from support to self-sufficiency? You walk a tightrope. You eventually work yourself off this one, but getting there will take massive doses of both support and self-sufficiency. You give lots of support for a long time. You teach lessons of self sufficiency as often as you can. You do both, good things for twenty or twenty-five years. You walk *the financial challenge* tightrope:

Support ——————————————————— Self-Sufficiency

If you don't, you neglect a fundamental role as a parent. You also ignore one of the predominant topics in the Bible, where God discusses money six times more often than he discusses prayer.

Many parents struggle when it comes to money and children. It is not uncommon for them to live with gaps on both ends of the continuum. The problem on the support end: parents who over-support their kids, continue to prop them up financially, let them live in their home interminably—rescuing all over again. The problem with self-sufficiency: parents who lack focus on what it will really take for kids to end up being ready to support themselves, especially in a world with occasional job scarcity, rising prices, and the intricacies of banking, insurance, investment, retirement, and property ownership.

You can stay on this tightrope, though. If you are willing to expend a little bit of effort, you can engage your kids in some basic principles of healthy money management. It is a process similar to how we teach kids about principles by which to live your life: the Ten Commandments, which were intended by God for our good. We need to reckon with what might be called "The Ten Commandments of Financial Readiness."

Commandment 1: Start Early

There is no time to lose in getting children ready for their economic future. Most parents can start the process earlier than they think.

For example, you can help a child associate work with earning, and earning with work. When you do this, you reinforce a basic lesson from the last chapter, 2 Thessalonians 3:10: "If a man will not work, he shall not eat." This is not meant to be an unduly harsh version of "singing for your supper." Rather, it is about the basic economics we started hearing in junior high school, that there is no free lunch.

A simple way to start: create paying and nonpaying jobs for which children receive pocket change for compensation. Our approach was to get Phil, Mark, and Tim involved in simple household chores, such as setting the table, clearing it, and emptying the dishwasher (most of our job assignments come in threes to keep everyone engaged). Doing the work led to payday, when they got a buck or two, money they could spend as they saw fit.

Over time we expanded the duties and increased the pay, so they could continue to correlate work and money. They have plenty of chores to do that are simply part of being in our household, so they don't get paid for everything. And like typical parents we have paid early, often, and in abundance to get them through their childhood. Nonetheless, we have elected to use some of their work around the house as a training ground for how support becomes self-sufficiency.

They have collected the household trash and recycling items and taken it to the curb once or twice per week. Lynn has had them cleaning bathrooms, dusting tables, and vacuuming the house from the time they could do even a marginal job at the tasks. They each do most of their own laundry. We have made them take their turn at mowing the lawn, washing cars, and shoveling snow. Paydays are larger—and more anticipated!—as they have gotten older.

We hear from them regularly how lousy we are as parents to make them work as much as we do. They tell us from time to time how *all* the *other* parents (the good ones, not bad ones like us) just give their kids the money they need. I respond by telling them how grateful they will be to have learned how to make it in our world economically. They hardly seem grateful, but we've stayed the course.

Now that they are approaching adulthood, we are reaching reality time, where we can look over the fence at the next era, when they will have to become self-funding and increasingly autonomous. We will still give them tons of support, in specified amounts, through the college years. But we have limited the support, so they have to increase their workloads if they are going to increase their earnings. Our goal is to prepare them for the costs of living the life they can only begin to imagine for themselves.

I am *not* saying there is a right or wrong way on this issue. We chose to do it one way. You may have a better approach. I am advocating you walk a path with your kids to get them started on tackling financial reality. It will benefit them to start early, so they do not build a false sense of how money works in our world.

Far too many parents tilt on the tightrope toward perpetual, long-term support all the way through high school and then seem surprised how unprepared their children are for the transition into adulthood. They blame the expense of making it in our society when kids "are forced to" live with them into their late twenties and thirties.

Does it cost a lot to reach self-sufficiency? No doubt about it. I can't help but wonder at how our lack of awareness of that cost reduces the parental action needed to start preparing our children for that reality. Part of your success in your kids' financial preparation will be to climb onto this tightrope sooner rather than later.

Commandment 2: Value Education

I was enjoying a cup of coffee with a couple I had just met one afternoon last month. They were about my age, but had started their family sooner, so their three children had made it through the college years. Since they had devoted most of their lives to ministry jobs, which are notoriously poor paying, I was surprised to hear them mention the names of major universities when they described each son or daughter's path to adulthood. I couldn't help but whine about the costs of college waiting just around the corner for me, which at first made them smile. "We thought it would be impossible too," they remarked, "but we found out that, if you have focused your kids on the value of education, and they will be diligent to navigate the system, schools will do everything they can to get them through the financial drain." Their words gave me some measure of comfort and quelled the whining, at least momentarily.

Let me give you some background on me. I grew up in what sociologists would call a "blue-collar" setting. My dad was a truck driver, drywaller, and maintenance man who worked extremely hard all his life, and my mom was a secretary because she needed to work if ends were going to meet. Yet it was a given that my sisters and I would attend college or get some form of education beyond high school, because our parents believed education was vital to our future well-being. By the time I obtained an undergraduate and professional degree, my experience bore out their belief.

I passed on that belief to my kids, with an exclamation point. I wanted them to grow up with a huge vision for what education means in a person's life. So, from the time they had the barest understanding about school, we started visiting college and university campuses whenever we could. Part of every vacation itinerary is to tour any school of significance wherever we are. As our boys have grown up, they have been on scores of campuses around the country. Phil, Mark, and Tim see college as where, not if.

The results I'm living with? I just spent a week in California touring five major universities Phil is considering. We're not sure if he'll actually pursue USC or UCLA, but he is not shy about shooting for the moon on school. No cheap proposition for me. And no whining either, because the dream we instilled in our kids is becoming a reality. Now I am banking on what my friends told me about wisely negotiating the coming years. We will get through it, and it will be worth it.

Really worth it. I mean that in financial terms. One of the most predictable values in our world is education. Parents and kids can't afford to ignore it. Your support of your children's educational future will be a key to their future self-sufficiency. Why? Income is quite predictable based on education. It is a numbers game, as you can see for yourself:

Median Annual Household Income, by Educational Attainment of Householder, 1997

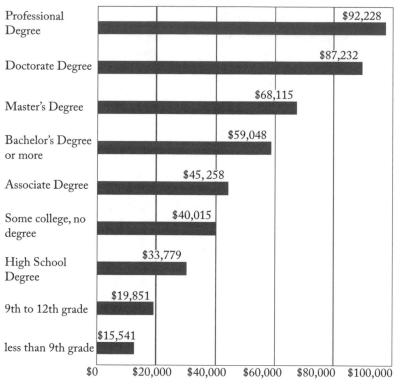

Professional Degree	$92,228
Doctorate Degree	$87,232
Master's Degree	$68,115
Bachelor's Degree or more	$59,048
Associate Degree	$45,258
Some college, no degree	$40,015
High School Degree	$33,779
9th to 12th grade	$19,851
less than 9th grade	$15,541

From Trends in College Pricing 1999, The College Board.[2]

The value of education is not just theoretical. It is much more real than most families realize. Quite simply, the failure to achieve self-sufficiency may be at stake.

Commandment 3: Experiment Often

It has been rumored that more United States citizens have worked for McDonald's than for any other company in the country, and I am one of them. It was my first official job. Little of my burger-flipping expertise translated into future employ-

134

ment, but the lessons I learned over those eighteen months about excellence, teamwork, customer service, process and procedure, efficiency, and diligence have served me to this day. So have all my subsequent jobs as a farm field hand, printer's assistant, construction laborer, school bus driver, delivery man, factory worker, assembler, janitor, librarian, and office clerk. Although these jobs had little to do with my ultimate professions, they taught me a lot about what I'm good at, what I'm passionate about, and what I can do to make a living.

The process of experimentation is more important to your child's financial future than you might think. Every young man or woman needs to wander a bit before they are going to be able to determine his or her future vocational path to self-sufficiency. You can be a guide along the way, supporting their choices to try a variety of jobs on for size.

Whenever I hear someone who is college-aged or beyond expressing uncertainty about what he or she really wants to do occupationally, I can't help but ask them about the variety of jobs they have tried. While there is no statistical tracking, there is a high correlation between long-term uncertainty and a deficit of experimentation and learning at younger ages.

This reality will be even truer in coming years. The employment landscape changes rapidly. Careers that didn't exist in prior generations can be the most available and the highest paying in the next. Being exposed to a wide variety of work experience will fuel more thoughtful and thorough consideration as they navigate their work life.

Commandment 4: Manage Income and Outgo

No matter where your children's education, experience, and job preferences take them, one thing is for sure: at some point, they will have some income to deal with. Managing that flow of funds is a critical factor in whether they move from your support to their own self-sufficiency. Their financial missteps may tilt you to the support end of the tightrope for longer than you'd like. You can avoid that one of two ways. Either you train them, or they drain you.

Kids will not wake up one day simply knowing how to create a budget and live within it.

I know it personally. By the time Lynn and I had finished college and grad school, we barely qualified for nursery school when it came to money management.

It wasn't for lack of good models. My parents used to arrange cash into budget envelopes every payday and lived well within their modest means. They were emulating my grandmother, who stretched my grandfather's meager pastor's salary by allocating their cash into glass jars into which the whole family could peek if they wanted a financial status update. It took us four university diplomas to become as smart as a far less educated grandmother from rural Indiana.

The backbreaking debt we had to face was a good teacher for us. Once we were no longer under water, we not only began to manage our income, we also resolved to do more for our boys than simply model good financial management. We got hands-on in teaching them how to budget their income and outgo, down to the nuts and bolts of creating, tracking, and reporting a financial plan.

The budget process started at age four. No kidding. We started them with the simple jobs and allowance I talked about earlier and then allocated their income into three areas: giving, saving, and spending. Each year they added more spending categories and increased income. Our goal was for them to allocate all income, from us or from their own jobs, to budgets representing their spending demands, including education, wardrobe, haircuts, gifts, entertainment, auto, and more. By the time they are sixteen, they live on a combination of our support and their earnings.

They have gotten very used to taking a pass on purchases due to empty accounts, to regretting impulse purchases that drained one of their budgets, and to finding extra work for something they really wanted. They can run their own reports on the computer program we've used and project how things will pan out financially in the months ahead based on choices they make. Our support is preparing them to manage their money when they have to be self-sufficient. It has been our job to educate them on the planning needed to use income wisely.

If you want some tools to get you started, the best ones we've found are *Master Your Money*[3] and *Raising Money-Smart Kids*[4] by Ron and Judy Blue. The Blues have made it their mission to help parents get on track with budgeting and planning, so they can do the training their children will need to survive adulthood.

Providing this gift to your kids is an indispensable part of walking the financial tightrope. Your support will be meaningful and constructive when it prepares them to plan wisely.

Commandment 5: Defer Gratification

Delaying anything is hard for a child. When it comes to money, it's hard for adults. Especially in our day. We live in circumstances where all we want, and then some, is readily available.

That is part of Gregg Easterbrook's point in his book *The Progress Paradox*.[5] Compare your lot in life to that of your great-grandparents and their parents before them. They would be astounded by what we have today: affordable, abundant food that allows for chronic obesity; college education as a standard expectation; medical care lengthening life spans by almost double; limitless communication and travel; and ubiquitous TVs, phones, and stereos that are supposed to satisfy us.

The paradox: when polled, Americans say they are no happier, and many of them feel disappointment and anxiety even though incomes have doubled in just one generation. Easterbrook cites several reasons for our discontentment. Satisfied expectations discourage people from thinking next year will be better, catalogues' glossy photos induce anxiety over what we don't have and cannot get, fears of financial collapse raise doubts whether our current standard of living will last, "abundance denial" has us thinking only those with double our income are well off, and too many options create overwhelming decisions. Ironically, although Easterbrook is a secular writer, he labels the ultimate cause "meaning want." In short, we wonder over life's purpose in the face of so many possessions.

The Bible calls this "the deceitfulness of money" in Mark 4:18–19: "Some people are like thorny soil. They hear the Bible's message, but it is quickly crowded out by the worries of this life and *the deceitfulness of money*" (my paraphrase and emphasis).

How do you beat deceit? Defer gratification. Children who become accustomed to readily satisfied whims will grow up a discontented lot. You have to say no more often than you might be right now.

In other words, help kids be satisfied with reasonable support—meeting basic needs and then some in all likelihood—so they arrive at some rational expectations of what they must have to sustain their own life when it is time. Their understanding of what it takes to be self-sufficient will be more within their reach once your support ends. The less you defer gratification, the higher their standards will become.

A paradox sets in when you defer gratification. It is the key, Easterbrook suggests, to gratitude. Once I overcome insatiable desire, I will become thankful for what I have, instead of anxious over what I don't possess. The fog obscuring my view clears. I can be grateful for God's best gifts: family and friends, health, and faith.

Commandment 6: Practice Generosity

Once you defer gratification, you are set up to pursue a practice that will assure money does not lay claim to the souls of your kids: giving. Teach your children to be openhanded, and cultivate a magnanimous spirit in them, and you can expect attitudes of generosity.

Jesus had a perspective-altering label for this: "Laying up treasures in heaven," he called it. He liked to talk about it using a colorful comparison. "Do not store up for yourselves treasures on earth, where moth and rust destroy," he instructed. "Store up for yourselves treasures in heaven, where moth and rust do not destroy."[6]

Jesus zings our conflicted point of view over giving. From our view heavenly treasure is (1) uncertain—how do we know for sure it is there? and (2) unimportant, because it lacks the urgency of all we face today. Jesus suggests we change the platform from which we look at money. From a heavenly view, he says earthly treasure is (1) uncertain because it does not outlast bugs and bacteria, and (2) unimportant when you simply put it to the moth and rust comparison test.

Holding on to our stuff will only sink its hooks into us. It clouds our ability to see our reality, as this reading suggests:

Blessings

If you woke up this morning with more health than illness, you are more blessed than the million who won't survive the week.

If you have never experienced the danger of battle, the loneliness of imprisonment, the agony of torture, or the pangs of starvation, you are ahead of 20 million people around the world.

If you attend a church meeting without fear of harassment, arrest, torture, or death, you are more blessed than almost three billion people in the world.

If you have food in your refrigerator, clothes on your back, a roof over your head and a place to sleep, you are richer than 75% of this world.

If you have money in the bank, in your wallet, and spare change in a dish someplace, you are among the top 8% of the world's wealthy.

If you hold up your head with a smile on your face and are truly thankful, you are blessed because the majority can, but most do not.

If you can read this message, you are more blessed than over two billion people in the world that cannot read anything at all.

You are so blessed in ways you may never even know.[7]

Unless and until we build this understanding in our children, the probability they will end up with generous hearts is slim. You teach them how to share by sharing yourself, and then you coach them on how to give.

Lynn and I learned this through the discipline of tithing, which our parents required of us to develop the habit of regularly allocating, even out of the most meager earnings, money we would share with our church and those in need. It is a practice we continued.

Our church helped us with a second idea, a year-end gift to meet international needs. We start the conversation with Phil, Mark, and Tim right after Thanksgiving so we have a month to decide what they will give out of their funds, and how we might pool our resources for greater impact. By Christmas we try to give until it hurts a little. Over many years we have been able to help the homeless, support an adoption center, present gifts to orphans, support missionaries, and supply bricks and labor to build church buildings.

Part of the financial test we parents face is to build the admirable character qualities our kids will need to handle their possessions well. Every time we do it, we parents are reminded that generosity is not just a good idea—it is the kind of character we want to have. Forming giving hearts is a challenge right up there with, say, walking a tightrope.

Commandment 7: Account for Personality

Chapter three highlighted the excellent work the Tiegers' book, *Nurture by Nature*, has done to adapt the study of temperament types to child rearing. A couple of years ago, they wrote *Do What You Are*,[8] a book designed to help parents and their children analyze career options. It is no ordinary job-assessment text, however, because rather than focus on job data or qualifications, it starts with the personality of your daughter or son, and leverages that information like a compass pointing to true north for *them*. Their point: many people end up hating their jobs, often because they do not really know themselves and have not considered their own temperament when making vocational choices.

This happens for a lot of reasons. Maybe the family business was their default choice. Perhaps their parents insisted they "do something practical." It might have been the path of least resistance at the time. But one thing is sure: their current job is a mismatch.

None of us wants that kind of future for our kids. We want them to bound out of bed in the morning, eager to get going on their day. If they could devote their working hours to what felt like their sweet spot, feel appreciated for what they do, get energized by it, love the people they work with, and hit the pillow at night filled with satisfaction each day, we would be thrilled for them. It can happen.

When you start early, value the education they will need, experiment often, and manage income, you plant them in a sort of economic greenhouse where you can watch their personality emerge. Pay attention and you will find clues about their future professional fulfillment. If your child is an extraverted, intuitive, analytical innovator, he or she probably shouldn't be pointed toward a career in accounting, banking, or the military. Likewise, an introverted, information-oriented, sensitive organizer will not likely find raving success starting a business, developing real estate, or marketing new products. It is not a matter of right and wrong. Their effectiveness won't tie to education or experience, either. There is a significant part of their future rooted in who they *are*.

As a parent, you can support them as they figure out how their temperament fits in different work environments. Beyond that, when you help them discover the unique ways they can impact our world, they are set for a lifetime of professional achievement.

It is easy to get distracted along the way by your own preferences, unfulfilled dreams, family business considerations, pressure from peers, short-sighted choices, and pragmatic needs. While some of those issues cannot be ignored completely, the more you can correlate career choice to personality, the more likely your kids are to build a vocational foundation that will lead to self-sufficiency.

Commandment 8: Identify Unique Gifting

God celebrates the individuality of each person. In Psalm 139:13–14, there are wonderful, poetic words about this distinctiveness: "For you created my inmost being; you knit me together in my mother's womb. I praise you because I am fearfully and wonderfully made." Romans 12:6 adds to the description: "We have different gifts, according to the grace given us." From the day of our conception we are being prepared for when our distinctiveness will find full expression by God's grace. God treasures our uniqueness.

How are you doing at treasuring your kids? We all have seen the hazards of moms or dads who try to squeeze their kids into ill-fitting molds. Parents play an indispensable role in coming alongside their children to help them understand who they are . . . and who they are *not*.

Candidly, the first part of that job, helping them see who they are, is easy by comparison. You can start with lists like those in the Bible. Romans 12:6–8, 1 Corinthians 12:7–11, Ephesians 4:11, and other passages, use terms like leaders, teachers, administrators, craftsmen and craftswomen. They tell us that some of our children will come with a bent toward mercy, wisdom, knowledge, hospitality, music, helping, encouragement, giving, faith, and/or discernment. Some of them will move into our world with a prophetic edge to them, an orientation toward shepherding or reclaiming those who have lost their way, or even a natural ability to pastor or plant churches. Bottom line: your son or daughter has two or three God-given gifts you had nothing to do with that they received whether they deserved them or not. Those gifts will make all the difference in their world if they understand them well.

Keep a list of these attributes handy, and be on the lookout for evidence of their presence in your child's life; then you can begin to identify where specific gifts are coming to light. Name them when you see a pattern develop. If you are unsure, you can ask others what they see, especially through the adolescent years. Beware of "false positives" when you might project something onto them you hope is there; that can be more confusing than helpful.

In fact, the harder part of your job is to help your kids see who they are *not*. We all want to express the ultimate kind of belief in our children, for sure.

Just the other day, my mom told me she thought I'd make a great president. As in president of the United States. She really thinks it is true. I'd be delusional to agree with her, but I appreciate the vote of confidence from someone that important to me.

You are that important to your son, to your daughter. Your undying belief matters.

Your value of and belief in them is what allows you to do the harder work of lovingly helping them see where their self-concept may be misdirected. I work every day with people who think they are leaders, teachers, or have an edge on wisdom, often because their parents and others not only affirmed them, but also failed to hold up a mirror so they would see what is real. Now the other adults they bump into are left with the job of "re-parenting" them in a way, helping them see the truth of what they are really good at, and what they should allow others to do.

You do not want that kind of a future for your child. Yours is the most strategic position from which to help them have an accurate picture of their gifts. Color it in fully, so they know well who they are. But show them the lines in the drawing God has made, so they feel freed from trying to be something they are not. The earlier they start to identify their gifts, the better. It is a form of support no kid can do without, and it will set them up to sustain their life and work for the long haul.

Commandment 9: Define Professional Passion

I was proud of how, when someone would talk about my dad as a drywall finisher or maintenance man, they would say, "He's a pro." It was a well-deserved accolade. My dad always did his work with zeal and excellence.

We use the term "professional" when we want to describe someone who does a job well, white- or blue-collar, paid or unpaid. That's how we want our kids to be known, don't we?

Defining professional excellence for them will push us past mere career planning and push us to find out what each daughter or son is really passionate about. It evokes the military recruiting line, "It's not just a job, it's an adventure." One of my mentors said it to me this way: "Find what you love to do, and you'll never have to work." When you can help a child identify the kinds of employment that will sustain their zeal for the long haul, you have set them up for self-sufficiency.

Be prepared for the early discussions over how they can make a living skateboarding, dressing up dolls, skiing, dancing, or grinding out screeching "gotta-be-a-rock-star" guitar chords. They may make it in sports, fashion, the arts, or music, so you can never dismiss those longings. The more you engage them, though, the better they will get at identifying things they love to do. Eventually a handful of ardent interests will surface that you can tap into constructively. Keeping your ear to the ground for those deeper points of satisfaction could make all the difference in their world.

In the meantime, while their passions surface, help them see how their work ethic and diligence can set them apart. Parents know a reality few kids want to face: showing up eager to work each day is a big deal. I've told my boys and employees many times, "I may not outsmart many people, but I will outwork most of them."

An adolescent who has acquired the learned behavior of conscientiousness will set high standards for professional excellence in the long run. You put that industrious attitude into someone who loves their work, and they will conquer their corner of the world!

Commandment 10: Understand Lifestyle Choice

In 1981, a new TV show hosted by a little known British gentleman named Robin Leach found its way onto our national stage; *Lifestyles of the Rich and Famous* tapped an unexpected interest. Although its run ended by the late '90s, it spawned a host of other shows devoted to revealing the lifestyles of celebrities notable for their wealth if nothing else, such as *It Is Good to Be* _____ (the diva of the week), *The Fabulous Life of* _____ (a sports celebrity or rock star), *Cribs* (an MTV version of The Parade of Homes), and the like.

145

These shows are more than a result of our voyeuristic interest in the famous: they have ignited the sense that theirs is the lifestyle we deserve. Today, you can't go long without a pitch for you to join those whose lifestyles set the standard for society. It's in our magazines, our malls, even our courtrooms. It's in our catalogues, our website favorites, our homes and gardens. You can have a dream life, if you'll buy the next lottery ticket, take the next vacation, make the next investment, own the next car, or do whatever gives you the life you deserve. Advertisers are expert at selling us the rich and famous lifestyle, even if we're not so rich and famous.

The result: skyrocketing consumer debt from $300 billion then to $1.8 trillion today, personal bankruptcy filings growing from 700,000 to 1.8 million in just ten years. Within those statistics you will find individuals gripped by finances out of control, dominated by fear over what will follow financial reversal, or plagued by chronic dissatisfaction. That is when you see financial choices for what they are. Most money issues are, in the end, only symptoms. What is the real issue? A person's often unwitting choice of lifestyle.

How do most people choose a lifestyle? They default to one of several options:

- Parents—Lynn and I moved into our marriage during college expecting the lifestyle our parents had after twenty-five years. That pattern is rampant today, especially when parents want to protect their kids from the harsh reality of what it is really like to be at the financial starting line.
- Friends—The Joneses still inspire our avarice and make understandable God's mandate, "Thou shalt not covet." We suspect that just past the fence lives precarious debt, but also wonder if we are missing an angle others have figured out. The only way off this treadmill is to declare the winner: them!

- Society—Monitor culture for a week and you see the truth of Romans 12:2: "Don't become so well adjusted to your culture that you fit into it without even thinking" (MESSAGE). It is hard to fight off well-tailored ad campaigns touting the lifestyle you *deserve*.

Your children will be no less influenced than you have been by parents, friends, society, and whatever else has shaped your sense of the standard of living you should have. They will either default to a lifestyle, or they will understand—because you focus them on the financial challenge they have—that their economic future is tied to the lifestyle they choose. If the standard of living they choose exceeds their ability to support it, guess who may foot the bill? You, unless you are able to tolerate the process of observing them in a chronic resource shortage.

Rather than let your kids default into a standard of living they cannot support, help them learn what really determines lifestyle. It starts with their *choices* regarding education and jobs. Based on the statistics mentioned already, unless they break the norms correlating the amount of schooling they do, the jobs they get, and the income they earn, the point where they stop pursuing further degrees or increase their job skills will determine their way of life. The starting point of economic reality is income, unless a rich uncle or lottery win helps you defy fiscal gravity.

There is a second dimension of lifestyle choice: your son or daughter's tastes or wants. Assume they marry sometime in their twenties. Between their spouse's tastes and their own wishes they will set some of their financial boundaries. Most people earn enough to pay for the basics such as food, shelter, clothing, and the like. Once those expenses are covered, money flows toward discretionary purchases.

That is where things get interesting. Why? Every person has one or two "points of insanity," things they will spend money on in amounts the rest of us see as crazy.

147

I'll give you an example. My wife can be insane when it comes to crafts. She will spend sums that would make your head spin, quicker than you can imagine. To her it makes all the sense in the world. If she has a spare dollar, she gladly devotes it to some sort of art form that will keep her hands busy.

After twenty-eight years of marriage, I still don't get it. But if I contest her point of insanity, she can quickly point out mine. One of them is dining out. I blanch at ten bucks spent on needlepoint while we're on our way to spend $50 on a meal. Makes perfect sense to me! What could be better than enjoying community over a good meal? It's insane when you think about it. And don't even get us started on motorcycles. On that subject, I admit to insanity.

I've counseled hundreds of couples and single parents about money issues, in pastoral, legal, small group, and personal settings. Every individual has points of insanity. It might not be art, food, or recreation, but it could be travel, cars, a house, pets, or even what they spend on their kids. Given an option, most people will even skimp on necessities if they can hoard a few more dollars to support their insane taste or want. The funds spent there reflect their choice of lifestyle.

A third lifestyle factor is circumstances. Sometimes your way of life is beyond your control. One of your children's lives may be hit by a storm, so their circumstances or needs dictate their financial future. The twist in the path might occur at any time.

When my parents were forced into early retirement by my dad's health, they eventually relocated to California where my sister Rhonda could help provide part of their care. A single teacher, she makes time for them like few adult children I've ever known. She has responded to the need gladly, and our whole family is grateful for how she has risen to the occasion.

But our family's circumstances have affected Rhonda's lifestyle. She has said no to some job opportunities when she could have earned more. She elects a lifestyle of care in the face of unanticipated circumstances.

Preparing your children to reckon with how education, tastes and wants, and circumstances and needs will affect their financial destiny is simply the smart thing to do. It will keep them from reacting passively when their life takes a twist.

One final factor will contribute to lifestyle choice: a child's sense of purpose or calling could have economic implications. God has transcendent purposes in mind for every person, one that is not about money, first and foremost. The apostle Paul describes it this way in Ephesians 4:1: "I urge you to live a life worthy of the calling you have received." At some point, your child may start to grasp that God has planted some sort of calling in their soul, a purpose that will drive their life choices. It may influence their income, though.

Lynn's sister and brother-in-law, Karin and Doug Allrich, realized early they were passionate about missions work. Twenty years into careers as a missionary nurse and pilot, respectively, they know how their calling affected their lifestyle. So do we, because Lynn manages their U.S. accounts while they live in Indonesia. Their sense of calling into missions has had financial and lifestyle implications. They have faced those consequences head-on and lived within their limited means with a sense of God's smile on their choice.

Many people become gripped by a desire to tackle a challenge bigger than them, but doing so means sacrifice. Regardless of education, tastes, wants, circumstances, or needs, their way of life will be dictated by their calling and how they respond to it. If they mismanage their resources, their ability to fulfill their purposes may be cut short. We saw it in Bible college when pre-seminary students bailed out on pastoral calling over mismanaged lifestyles. Businesspeople never quite got around to accomplishing a deep sense of what God wanted them to do with some of their time and money due to unnecessarily inflated standards of living.

The last thing you want for one of your kids is for them to miss out on their calling. However, you will have to ready them for fiscal reality so they can make the most of the adventure God has in store for them.

Do not allow your children to fall prey to a default lifestyle. Prepare them for self-sufficiency while they have the benefit of your support by keeping the issues surrounding their education, wants, needs, and calling on the front burner.

The Legacy

It has happened hundreds of times in my law office. A mom or dad calls a "time-out" on life to ponder their death. Lawyers euphemistically call it "estate planning." On the surface, anyway, it is about creating a will or trust, signing some documents, putting things in order. Without fail, the deeper truth bubbles up. Parents ponder what they are leaving to their children.

Most of them nobly wish to provide an inheritance that will leave their kids and grandkids in better financial shape than they might have been. However, when they actually start to do the math, when they picture the moment their daughter or their son receives a check for a specific sum of money, that is when they realize they have a legacy greater than money to leave them.

What happens with that money will not depend on the amount of the check. Whether an inheritance will enhance a child's life or destroy it comes down to how ready they are to receive it. There is little the parents can do at that moment, outside of putting some restrictions on it to account for how it might be squandered. Most of their legacy, financially anyway, will be bound up inside that child, and how ready they are to make good use of the last portion of support a parent gives them.

Gazing honestly at that moment is defining. How does it look to you? The rewards of facing the financial challenge well, seeing kids "get it" with money, watching their self-esteem grow when they do well at something, and sensing their vocational passion and purpose are among the most satisfying you can know as a parent. All it will take to get there is walking the financial tightrope.

7

Umbilical Cords, Apron Strings, and Phone Lines

The Interdependence Challenge

> When mothers talk about the depression of the empty nest, they're not mourning the passing of all those wet towels on the floor, or the music that numbs your teeth, or even the bottle of capless shampoo dribbling down the shower drain. They're upset because they've gone from supervisor of a child's life to a spectator. It's like being the vice president of the United States.[1]
>
> Erma Bombeck

I was in my thirties before I heard about it. It went something like this. "Individuation," the Christian psychologist said, "is the last task of a parent. Unless and until a child 'individuates'—becomes their own individual, autonomous person—they are not yet an adult. They must move out from under their parents, not for the purpose of assuming a position over them, but to become their peer. When individuation happens well, it maintains the attachment first formed in the womb."

Huh? How does a person become "autonomous," by definition independent or free, and maintain "attachment," which means dependence and emotional involvement? I didn't know it at the time, but another tightrope walk was shaping up. It is one that poses the final challenge for those parents willing to live with tension to our last "official" day.

None of us are sure what constitutes the finish line for a dad or mom, at least the point at which we cut apron strings so our kids can get on with adulthood. Our oldest turned eighteen this year. The law says he is an adult. We're done, in theory. We are more connected than ever in many ways, through college tuition liabilities if nothing else.

I have watched numerous friends navigate their children's passage into adulthood before me. When I've talked to them about it, they describe the mix of joy and pain that accompanies this era of life. Certain events bring poignant moments, where the separation is real. Author Bruce Cameron describes the day he took his first daughter to college this way:

> When I took my older daughter to college, I was so focused on the logistical task of moving her belongings, I didn't really think about what I was *really* doing: moving her out of my life and into the start of hers. After spending the last half decade prowling the house at night, wondering where she was and what she was doing and with whom she was doing it, we were now entering a phase where I would never know these things. No curfew, no way to [screen] her dates, no opportunity to offer constructive criticism when needed, which was, in my opinion, constantly.
>
> Looking at my daughter, I saw my little girl in a woman's body, tall and strong but unfinished, not ready. Or maybe it was I who was not ready—I certainly felt unsure as she

walked us to the parking lot for the final good-bye. How was this natural, to drive my daughter to this strange place, write fifty checks, and then drive away, leaving her in the hands of strangers with whom I shared nothing but the contents of my bank account? Her whole life I had protected her from harm, a job that did not in any way feel done.

And then we were there by the car. My wife hugged her and sobbed as if our daughter were leaving on a boat for the New World. . . . When it was my turn I pulled her to me and concentrated on remaining dry eyed. The words I wanted to say could not fight their way past the tight constriction in my throat, and when I felt the press of her lips against my cheek, I had to look away.

I did manage to say something, I think, before sliding numbly into the front seat and starting the minivan. My daughter's little wave was harder for me than the last hug. . . . I found myself remembering her waving at me from the front window when I would leave for work in the morning, when she was not just my first but my only child.

My wife and I didn't talk much on the way home. . . . We were entering a new phase of life now, the start of a process of letting our children go. . . . "I miss her already," my wife murmured after a bit. I did too. . . .

Then the cell phone rang. My wife answered it, since we have a policy against me crashing the car while I'm driving it. "Oh, honey," my wife said after a moment. "I understand. I know it can be difficult." I sent her a questioning look, and she made a sad face. "I'm sure you'll be okay, dear," she responded after a long silence. "Honestly, it is going to be all right." . . .

My wife hung up with a thoughtful look on her face. "Is our college girl homesick already?" I asked sympathetically. . . . "No. She says she's the only person in her dorm without a credit card." "Oh," I answered. . . . "She thinks this is somehow something that I'm supposed to fix?" "Of course," my wife answered smoothly. "You're the father."[2]

155

A Mother's (and Father's) Work Is Never Done

Even after those first steps toward independence, you are still the father, still the mother. You've built deep bonds for a couple of decades, only to set the stage for the emotional independence that feels like the tearing of the fabric of connection. It will take years to happen. You will hang on too tightly for too long sometimes. Your kids will feel abandoned and pull in close for a season, only to push you away. You will wonder who is crazier, them or you.

William Bridges wrote *Transitions: Making Sense of Life's Changes,* a best seller on navigating change in life, including this one. He describes this transition as "establishing a separate identity, distinct from that of so-and-so's child."[3] He suggests this phase begins in adolescence around various rites of passage such as first jobs, driving, graduations, and so on, and it is not uncommon for this phase to last into the child's thirties.

The ideal is to end old dependencies and establish the person formerly known for being your child as a separate social entity. Parents and children move *beyond* that separateness to something more complex, what Bridges calls a "deeper sense of interrelatedness."

You are both walking a tightrope called *the interdependence challenge.* You continue building the bonds formed over your years of investing in a child. And then, without letting up one ounce of attachment, you cut them loose so they can move toward autonomy. You are neither dependent nor independent. You are interdependent. This tightrope will leave you feeling pulled by two good things for the rest of your lives:

Attachment ———————————————— Autonomy

I like how the book of Proverbs describes interdependence in a family who can manage this tension well. Proverbs 31:28 speaks of moms: "Her children arise and call her blessed." Proverbs 23:24 covers dads: "The father of a righteous man has great joy." Children take the spotlight in Proverbs 17:6: "Parents are the pride of their children." It provides a composite picture of moms and dads and kids ending up in a place where they know what it means to be dependent *and* independent, bonded *and* individuated, attached *and* autonomous.

The problem end of the tightrope is usually the autonomous side—holding on too tightly. You have seen what happens when a parent or adult child tilts the balance too far to the dependence side. Mom cannot let go of past relating patterns and gets easily hurt if she doesn't receive her quota of phone calls or letters. A dad finds no man acceptable for his "little" girl and withholds approval for a marriage that is by no means a sure thing, but needs his blessing. Kids keep phoning home for money, decision sign-offs, or squatter's rights to a bedroom they should have permanently vacated a decade ago.

It's not like there are *right* answers to any of these situations, though. That is what makes parenting a challenge, all the way to the end. At best we manage another tension, perhaps better if we are aware of the polarities pulling at us. Balancing attachment and autonomy—doing *both*—is going to be one thing: hard. It's another tightrope.

Parenting for the Long Haul

Keeping your balance as children move toward interdependence can be accomplished, though. You can end up with the picture in Proverbs of long-term relationship.

Since I have only recently arrived at this stage, I performed an unscientific but fascinating poll of people I know at all phases of this transition. I was interested not only in their experiences as parents who have run this gauntlet, but also their reflections on what they have seen others (including their own parents) do well—and poorly—in walking the interdependence tightrope. My survey resulted in a simple collection of a few basic ideas to make this part of parenting incredibly easy! Right . . .

The discussions actually produced a longer list than I expected of a wide variety of challenging things you will have to do well, things that represent one or both of the polarities. And you will rarely be sure how it will all pan out in the end. But parent you must, all the way to that ill-defined finish line.

Do the Process in Stages

The "Reader's Digest Condensed Version" of what you will need to do is this: force yourself to face the stages of increased independence, where you refuse to bail them out or intervene, and instead become a mentor and guide to your child. Bridges's *Transitions* concepts are helpful here, because he helps you see the three phases of any transition. He describes transitions as always moving through (1) the old, (2) the in-between, and (3) the new.

We all have a sense of the old. Those are the routines, even ruts, we've found within our relationship with our daughter or son. We all tend to hang on to the old. A child's room remains their room, often decorated to late junior high school tastes. They assume they will always have their place, sometimes returning to it now and then for another decade or so.

The new is the emerging reality, ultimately all the different ways you will relate peer to peer, but it can be hard to get there. Most people either refuse to face the new, or they handle transition by jumping to the new too abruptly. They regard the change like a switch to be flipped without warning. But like a sudden surge of voltage through an electric line blows circuit breakers, too quick a shift to the new throws both parents and children for a loop.

That is why we need an "in-between." The in-between phase of any transition is the place where we reflect on the old, recount the good things we experienced, regret what disappointed us, and grieve the losses associated with having to let go or with what was. An in-between space also allows us room to anticipate the future, plan the contours we want "the new" to feature, and determine how and when we will take on the responsibilities associated with going forward.

There is a problem with the in-between, though, Bridges points out: it tends to be a chaotic, disorienting no-man's-land. The discomfort of letting go of what is familiar—the past—and the premature leap to the excitement of what is ahead—the future—tends to dislodge us from the in-between, a zone we would be wise to dwell in for a season. We lag behind to avoid change, or we spring into action to dodge processing it. The better response: devote some time to hanging around the in-between. It will give us space to ponder, enjoy, and grieve what we are letting go. The in-between will prepare us for where we are going. The old and the new are made more meaningful by the in-between.

You will need to envision how the new and the in-between affect your world, your child, your parenting. How will you fully drink in what was? What shape do you envision for what will be? The stages of change you experience in this era will be the in-between.

Create Rites of Passage

One way to mark various stages is to carve out events that will signal change. I experienced this firsthand with my parents. The day after graduating high school meant adventure for me: a six-week missions trip to Europe. I joined a team of thirty students who pitched tents on the lawn of an Austrian youth camp where we did construction work for the summer.

The trip meant a lot to me and my personal growth, but it became a rite of passage too. My parents used the experience as a proving ground for my ability to take on adult responsibility. The midnight curfew I lived with before I left evaporated on my return. Reporting my whereabouts beforehand? It became a morning-after debrief. Planning for college start-up was my

159

deal. They figured that if I could survive six weeks in Europe on my own, I could be more responsible for myself at home.

Many cultures have rites of passage into adulthood—the bar or bat mitzvah, the ancient hunt, or other ceremonial baton passes—but ours doesn't. You can create some of them as early as age twelve. One of my friends assembled a group of men who were his best friends when each of his sons turned fourteen for a blessing ceremony, where they marked the beginning of high school as a move to manhood. Some passage rites will be formal, due to a graduation or departure for college. I know one family who celebrates those days by presenting each child with a "Certificate of Independence," in which they express their confidence for a bright future of ongoing growth into adulthood. It may be a marriage or first baby. Rites of passage come whenever you deem a life event pivotal enough to mark a moment of increased autonomy.

Allow for Mistakes

"All learning comes from failed experience," the speaker said. He was training trainers, those who are supposed to be sure people learn what they are trying to teach. But he was making us face the inclination to think that saying it is enough.

His point: unless students get to try what you're teaching, they won't sense the urgency that comes when you make mistakes. It's like the difference between driver's education in the classroom and actually being behind the wheel; until you nearly crash you don't become a real driver.

What is true for drivers is true for children. The older they get, the more likely their lessons will come from failure. Failure you want to save them from!

Letting go means you will have to move over to the passenger's seat so they can take the controls of their life. Wear your seat belt. It will be perilous while they gain the experience for living their own life. Beware of your unwillingness

160

to let go. You may have a harder time letting go than your kids do leaving.

They may dress weird (will it be any worse than some of your old outfits?), pierce parts of their body, and tattoo skin, only to regret it later. Will your shame really help the situation? If they defer college for a while, take a job you know is ill-advised, or bungee jump off cliffs, you may have to hold your breath, pray, and hope for the best. They have to learn, often via their own experiences of embarrassment, frustration, disappointment, regret . . . *failure*. Whether you want them to or not, they will make mistakes.

In the end, parenting is not about you. It is about your children living the life they choose, enduring a sort of failure quota; making a reasonable number of mistakes comes with the territory. There is no other way to learn.

Deal with Your Differences

Wouldn't it be nice if there was a one-size-fits-all way to hit the finish line to child rearing? But you can anticipate variety here too.

You will experience differences based on gender. Moms process the tension between attachment and autonomy differently than dads. Boys will have to transition with mom, and girls with dad. How that works will be different than how girls move away from their mother, and how boys separate from a father. Temperament or personality differences will come into play again. Thinkers and feelers, structured and unstructured types respond to change differently.

Differences will also show up based on how a parent historically engaged with the child. Stay-at-home moms will differ from fathers who worked too much, and dads with a home office will process change unlike a professional, working mother.

Another factor will be differences between kids. We marvel at how unique each of our kids can be despite having been fished

161

out of the same gene pool. Those distinctions will show up in significant ways when the major shift of adulthood comes.

Your family will probably experience honest differences of opinion about how to move from the old to the new, between the parents, the kids, and the parents and kids. Since there are no right and wrong answers on how to get through this era—only principles to keep you from losing your balance—you will have to compare notes often and find the way to build interdependence *together.*

Focus on What Matters Most

As your kids get older, especially beyond age eighteen, the range of issues over which you will have input narrows dramatically. Your longing for attachment, a good thing, may expose itself in attempts to control. Autonomy means you hold your breath, close your eyes, and hope for the best . . . most of the time. You still want to weigh in, perhaps heavily, on occasion.

I have a friend who made just one issue—their children's choice of spouse—the sole decision on which he and his wife would continue to grip tightly once their kids hit college. Since they released their hold on other issues, their two sons tolerated the intrusion well. The boys were in their twenties when they were actively courting, and dad and mom knew they couldn't break up any relationship. But they were not shy about praying intently over the choice, engaging as much as they could, even speaking honestly about their opinions.

There are a handful of make or break decisions your daughter or son will make. Have you determined which ones matter most? Those few get the focus of your attachment; on everything else, tilt toward autonomy.

Maintain Selected Traditions

Family rhythms and routines help to define its bonds; they are one of the reasons why it feels good to be part of a family unit. You become comfortable with the way things are, especially during holidays, at birthdays or anniversaries, or on family vacations. When it comes time to camp out more on the autonomy end of the continuum, part of your disorientation will result from having to begin to let go of the traditions that symbolized what it meant to be part of your family.

Some parents react to the confusion by throwing in the towel of tradition. You don't have to. You simply need to be a bit more strategic. Figure out what "anchors" will survive into the new day.

A few of them may echo your past traditions. If your family lives close, you could still gather for birthday celebrations, and they become part of the new rhythms of extended family. One family we know maintained a system of Christmas gift giving as a way of staying connected: a competition to see who can give the funniest present. It keeps them on the lookout 24/7/365 for the winning gift. This tradition maintains and signifies their ongoing affection.

You may need to springboard from old practices into new patterns. How you did family vacations may become a place or platform for family reunions or trips. You get the idea. You will have to experiment to see what takes root, and those anchors will keep your family leaning into each other.

Strengthen Your Marriage

A home with no kids leaves mom and dad now facing each other. Plenty of couples do not make it past this stage because they don't have much of a relationship outside of their joint project to raise their kids. Are you ready?

You cannot afford to wait until the last child exits to figure it out. Some children keep coming back home to live even though they are twentysomething, thirtysomething, or fortysomething because parents don't know how to function without children as gears in the household machinery. That is not fair to you or

163

your kids. The bottom line: you may need to seek the marriage counseling you have avoided for too many years.

Having devoted a lot of time and money in our counseling, we are twenty-eight years into a marriage that has not always been easy. It has taken a lot of work; the payoff is enormous, though. We are looking *forward* to the days of increasing freedom when we can focus on each other. We sometimes say to our kids, when they mock how much we're in love, "Don't let the door hit you on the way out!" We have a strong incentive to get our boys living on their own so we can enjoy the life we have built together, independent of our life as parents.

Anticipate Extra Time

The marital reality coming your way will touch the rest of your life too. What are you going to do with the time you have on your hands? I am beginning to experience what I've observed in many other parents: whether mom stayed at home, dad attended events, or the family chased every spare minute out of the calendar with activities, you will be shocked at the vacuum that hits your calendar when all that ends.

This chaos can be turned into your greatest ally. Most people harbor some unfulfilled dream they never got to pursue. While it is too late to be a major league shortstop or lead ballerina, there are probably a few wishes you sidelined in favor of your kids. It may be time to resurrect one or two of them.

You do have time. Not just in your calendar. In your life. Many moms and dads are fifty, give or take a few years, when the nest empties. Assuming reasonably good health, you still have twenty or thirty years to mark our world. It is not time to just grind it out to retirement, or slip into some neutral gear. And you can't simply maintain your old level of attachment to your kids.

You may make more strides in the new day than ever before. I take great hope from Mike Wallace. Regardless of your opinion of CBS's *60 Minutes* anchor, he is still going strong well into his eighties. He did not even start on the show until he was past fifty. His greatest professional achievement hadn't even been conceived until after his children were long grown.

What if your time and achievements transcended good professional or educational pursuits into eternal payoffs? Perhaps it is time to experiment with increased discipleship, study, or solitude. Maybe you could help some compassion ministries get the job done locally, nationally, or even internationally. Don't squander what could be a rich, rewarding season of impact!

You still have the time to make some great things happen in your life. But a lot of where you go and what you do will be defined by time. Your time. And how you invest it as it becomes more available. Do not squander the opportunity.

Name the Tension

Maintaining the balance between attachment and autonomy will create moments of awkwardness you never anticipated. Being aware of the extremes will help you live with some of them. However, some of those moments need to be named. When tension starts to crop up, don't let it go underground. Try to anticipate which issues tend to create long-term discomfort.

One way to identify something needing discussion is to project how things today will feel when you roll the calendar forward ten or twenty years. If your relating patterns are going to be strained over the long haul because of a subsurface issue, you should talk about it sooner rather than later.

For example, a married child tells mom or dad about marital discord, but mandates no conversation about it with the spouse, so now everyone has to live with a little pretense. Unannounced drop-ins become a rub, and yet their increasing frequency is tolerated without a word. A mild annoyance is turning into a

165

long-term grudge, but, like most people, you don't like conflict, so you live with it rather than confront it.

These tensions will fester into relational wedges—wedges you do not have to tolerate. Get help if you don't have intact communication patterns. But do not destroy lifetime attachments over issues you should put on the table and resolve. Life is too short, and family too valuable, for tension to push people farther apart than they should be.

Refuse to Be a Victim

"You nevah call your mothah. What is wrrooong with you?" So goes the caricature painted by stand-up comedians. It is not so funny when you see parents bury hurt feelings under a heap of growing, silent resentment, only to later leak toxic hurt and shame.

My mom and I had to duke this one out. We went through an era when I dropped the ball on adequate connection with my folks. Busy work, vigorous ministry, and a manic family schedule distracted me from even a threshold compliance with the "Honor your parents" mandate from the Ten Commandments.

To my mother's credit, she started out nagging but recovered to name the tension. Rather than feel like a victim of my choices, she kindly described how she and my dad were feeling ignored. It was true, so I had to admit their feelings were warranted.

Beyond that, she stated what she wanted: phone calls every week or two, and an annual flight by me from Chicago to San Francisco, where they live. That was easy enough for me, and it is something I've built into my life over the years since then. In some ways my mom simply applied the lessons of chapter 5. She continued to *clearly state* her views on issues, behaviors, and consequences, and that gave me room to do the same.

The conversation also allowed me to point out how the phone line works two ways. In order to make her feel more inclined to call me, I made sure she had the number for my ever-present cell phone—my umbilical cord to the world—on her speed dial. That one conversation, and those simple steps, moved everyone beyond feeling like victims of each other's behavior.

Don't let yourself slip into victim status. Have your antenna up for any sense you are being wounded by one of your children. Before you confront your child, you may decide your feelings are a clue that you are walking the tightrope between attachment and autonomy. It may require more, though, if something needs to change to keep better balance.

Reckon with Your Mistakes

You made some mistakes as a parent. Have you admitted that? Which specific errors have you owned up to?

We have benefited greatly from the good Christian counselors who have helped us be OK with being less than perfect. In fact, we have a standard reply to our kids' complaints: "That's something you'll have to work out in therapy. Come and talk to us then!"

We know a day is coming when they will. Our own wounds and shortcomings have inflicted a certain amount of damage they will have to account for later in life. When they do—and we hope they will face their issues head-on when they emerge—the ball will be in our court to deal with our part of it.

An observation: too many parents have a stake in maintaining their own innocence. They seem to feel that, if they admit to any mistakes, they will slide down the slippery slope to the conclusion that they failed in child rearing. They prop up an illusion that they got it all right or dismissively respond, "Well, we did the best we could."

That is an inadequate response to real issues your children have to process. You don't have to take the blame for everything or conclude that you were an abject failure as a parent.

167

But you do have to admit that some parts of your attachment were less than perfect.

You will need to engage constructively in a process of frank conversation. It will mean enduring the "tunnel of chaos" M. Scott Peck describes when we deal with what eats at true community. When you will let down your defenses, really listen to and hear your children, and own what you should, you can make your way through it. On the other side of such chaos lies a truer sense of bonding with which both parent and child can move into the future.

Reverse the Tide

Some parents make mistakes from which it may take a long time to recover. It is regrettable, but the long-term effects of workaholism, the consequences of substance abuse, patterns of emotional manipulation, separation through a divorce, or other life trauma may create distance with one or more of your children. They may grieve their losses and be content where your relationship is. However, if given the chance, they might opt for a deeper relationship with you. If that is your situation, you will need to take more initiative.

The good news: it is never too late for most children. Your kids may only be an "I'm sorry" away. What they need most is for you to recognize the issue and own your responsibility for it. Over time, then, they will rebuild old attachments or re-create the bonding you both missed.

It won't necessarily be easy. They may reject your overtures at first. Or they might respond positively at first, but then realize they need more time to rebuild healthy relating patterns due to the wounds you inflicted. Over time, however, you may recoup losses you created with them.

Get help if you need it. You may have a pastor, friend, or family member who knows how to mediate a reconciliation process. Reclaim lost time if you can.

Move from Mom to Mentor and Dad to Discipler

I grew up in the home of a Navigator, but not of seagoing vessels. I'm referring to someone affiliated with The Navigators, a Christian organization known as the eat-nails-for-breakfast group of discipleship kingpins. They take the spiritual development process seriously, as reflected in an extremely valuable series of curricula and methods designed to intensify the trend line of a person's growth.

My dad met Christ in the U.S. Navy through the Navigators and exploded in his maturity as a new Christian by following their routines of Bible study and memorization, prayer, and one-to-one and group mentoring. I had a front-row seat for twenty years of my dad as the discipler extraordinaire.

The shift from spectator to participant happened when I was in college, when my dad took me through the process. We would meet each week in his office—since he was a maintenance man his office was a broken down desk and creaky set of chairs buried in the corner of a storage room we shared with mops, wash buckets, and piles of floor wax canisters. We devoted a year to weekly study and accountability sessions. I experienced an unprecedented spurt of spiritual growth, Dad invested his life in yet another Christ-follower, and we moved into a new era of our relationship.

There comes a time when you move from mom to mentor, from father to facilitator. As your child gains independence, you counsel rather than correct, you guide rather than give direction, you consult rather than cure a child's mistake. Your relationship might not take on the formality my dad used with me, but the picture remains the same. Children gain autonomy when parents shift the focus of their input from directive to advisory.

Build Your Adult Relationships

There is nothing like a shared passion to bond people together, is there? Most of the time, those who have an obsession

169

in common end up spending lots of time together, and they build memories others don't share. They attend the theater together, play in regular golf foursomes, quilt or craft together, catch fish or hunt, drink lots of coffee while hanging out at Starbucks, jam with rock, jazz, or classical instruments, or tour new travel destinations. Mutual passion breeds shared life.

My friend Rich was in his late fifties when he decided to start motorcycling for one simple reason: his two grown sons did it. They had an OK relationship before, but it was nothing compared to how it blossomed during long bike trips across the United States. Rich, still biking into his seventies, would tell you the bonds he had with his sons grew more than ever before after they had left home. All because of motorcycles, their shared passion.

Even if your interests don't seem to mesh, keep a creative focus on building a relationship with your adult son or daughter. See where what you love most intersects, and see if it might be the ticket to deepened affection later in your life together.

Just Say No

Certain moments of truth will reveal the level of autonomy your family has reached: you refuse the invitation to Thanksgiving because you have your own plans, or one of your kids wrecks your Easter tradition because of their conflicting spring vacation plans. Those signals of change from the old to the new, while they create a little disequilibrium, are healthy. They announce that the in-between passage from old attachments to autonomous relating patterns has begun.

Since some of them are inevitable, you may want to think ahead, planning when it makes sense to turn this relational corner. Again, there are no right ways or times to do this. You have to decide what will keep you on the tightrope, navigating your way to independence. A well-timed "no," perhaps with aboveboard communication about everybody's need to move out of old routines, could be the best thing for your family.

Learn to Share

Regardless of whether you choose them, some of those transition points will be forced on you. Your son or daughter will likely marry someday, and then most holidays, vacations, and birthdays will test how well you learned the first lesson of kindergarten. Can you play well with others?

In-laws can become outlaws when families blend. If parents do not share well, Christmas becomes a dreaded source of tension. Competition for time and attention turns normal families into Hatfields and McCoys. A better alternative: take note of which events trigger the need to share, and then take initiative to talk through win-win solutions or schedules.

You may find yourself swallowing hard when you have to share your child with a new daughter- or son-in-law. Their youth or immaturity may trigger possessiveness, jealousy, and petty behavior. And that just describes your reaction! Any failure to intercept their shallow responses robs you of the promise a new relationship can bring.

You are still the parent. The onus is on you to learn to share. A rule of thumb: parents are sharing well when they move from feeling loss when they have to divvy up time with their child with others, to feeling gain because they love that new spouse and welcome him or her as their own child. Will it be hard? Sometimes, depending on where you are emotionally, and who your kids marry. Will it take time? Probably, because there are no formulas for living in the new day.

Monitor "The Grandparent Effect"

It may be true that the best thing about grandkids is spoiling them before you send them home. Those who have passed into the grandparent zone know it's not quite that simple.

171

Sharing your kids with extended family is one thing. The first baby one of your children bears will introduce three families—yours, your child's, and their in-laws—to a matrix of complexity requiring everyone to do a new balancing act. You will not leave this new phase of tightrope walking soon.

You may instantly begin to bond to a grandchild to some degree, and it may trigger old memories from a couple of decades before. But your kids need to have their family, do their parenting, establish their patterns. That won't mean complete autonomy, though. You may sometimes feel like the default babysitter, but you probably need to be there for more than that. It is simply hard to know exactly when that is. Right answers? Not anytime soon.

One invaluable role you can play in the midst of negotiating what works best for your family is to be more cheerleader than quarterback. Your adult children need to run the plays they deem best. You can encourage them whether they are winning at the moment or need to change their game plan to succeed. Do not underestimate how heartened other confused parents, especially those new to the tightrope, become when you cheer them on.

Be a Supporter, Not a Savior

How do you play it when chaos hits your adult children? What if it comes because they made bad choices, contrary to your counsel? You may be able to make the hurt go away, but should withhold help . . . maybe. How do you know?

Seek lots of wisdom, for starters. Most of the complications coming your children's way as they get older are more entangling than you will see at first blush. There is always more to the story than you hear at first. When a son or daughter's life takes a turn for the worse, you have to step into it gingerly.

One of the best things you can do is help them think of how *they* should handle *their* situation. The phone rang late one night at a friend's home. His sophomore son was calling to say he was quitting college. They flew him home for a triage session, and over the weekend that ensued figured out his dislike of school was due to underperformance in several classes.

They started imagining together what would happen if he dropped out. That would mean full-time work. What if the son treated school the same way, "working" forty hours per week at it? To add a little accountability, they signed an employment contract (literally) under which the son paid his dad $10 per hour in any week he devoted less than a full forty hours to studies. The son went back to school, never paid a dollar, and became a straight-A student.

Dad didn't save the day, he supported. And a crisis turned into a life lesson. That is what your kids need more than your salvage operation.

Be Clear on Financial Arrangements

The story is typical. Adult child needs money. Mom has money. Mom "loans" money to child. Child never repays. Mom gets mad. Mom suffers in silence. Child squirms when mom is around. Child avoids being with mom. Other siblings get mad when they find out about the loan.

You can play banker for your child, but play it like a banker. I have sat in law offices unwinding years of monetary transactions, in pastoral offices counseling families through breakdowns tied to inadvisable loans and gifts, and in small group circles helping drained parents live with shortfalls created by well-intentioned generosity. Financial entanglements can destroy otherwise healthy families. Resentments among kids rise. Parents and their children can't relate normally because money has tainted their future.

If you are in a family business, the stakes go even higher. Be clear on how you will work together at various stages, how the handoff of the business will occur, how you will establish

173

both real and perceived equity with any children who are not in the business. Just as money can make you "gain the whole world and lose your soul,"[4] you can gain a business partner and lose your family.

There are lawyers, accountants, and consultants who specialize in helping families plot a course when it comes to business matters. This is one of those arenas where you would do well to heed Proverbs 15:22: "Plans fail for lack of counsel, but with many advisors they succeed." Do not go it alone when the stakes are so high.

Communicate Estate Plans

One of the final indications of your unique attachment to children is the inheritance you leave them when you pass from this world to the next. A parent's death, however, redefines autonomy for a child. No wonder these extremes conspire to create unprecedented family conflict. Some families save their biggest fights for their parents' final days or death.

One part of finishing well as a parent is to save your family from a late-in-life fight that tears down all you've invested—not just financially, but relationally. Simple inattention, neglect, or bad planning can be enough to set the stage, which would be especially tragic, because of the ease with which you can avoid it.

There are a handful of official documents you can put in place to prepare your family for the end of your run:

- *Durable Power of Attorney for Health Care:* Appoints someone to make decisions about your medical treatment in the event you are incapacitated.
- *Durable Power of Attorney for Property:* Designates a representative, either a person or corporate trustee, to manage your financial affairs upon your disability.

- *Living Will:* States your wishes regarding discontinuation of heroic efforts to sustain life in the event your treating physician needs an advance medical directive.
- *Revocable Living Trust:* Creates a legal entity that outlives you; by transferring your property to it during your lifetime, it becomes the vehicle through which you distribute your property upon death, avoiding the court-based probate process. In addition to easing the estate administration process, your affairs are more likely to be kept private, and you can enhance the flexibility you give your designated trustee.
- *Will:* If you create a revocable living trust, your will simply appoints a guardian for minor children and then "pours over" any property left over into your trust. It is still a good idea to have a will even if you don't have a trust as a means to appoint guardians and distribute property.

Once you put these few building blocks in place, you can add other elements that make sense in light of your tax, family, business, and charitable concerns. Once you have settled on the right mix of documents and strategies, periodic updates will be required. It is never too soon to make this a first order of business.

As you make changes, let your kids know how you have provided for them. Lack of communication can only breed needless concern. Short-term chaos—a frequent fear that is rarely realized—over what you might disclose is a worthwhile price to pay for long-term peace.

The No-Finish Finish Line

Now that you have read through this compilation of what awaits you *after* your kids are grown and gone, you most likely realize that complexities with kids never end. Parenting never ends, really.

175

At most, your children move to a new stage of relationship with you, one that will find an ironic end. Depending on the course your life takes, you will lean back on them in ways that give back your own autonomy. It will be more needed than ever for this generation, due to lengthening life expectancies and advances in medical treatment. The blessing of advanced years often comes with a need for a new era of dependence and attachment, but now you are leaning on them like they once leaned on you.

Wise parents treat the coming days like a seasoned investor. Today's relational deposits form a reservoir you will draw on when you can no longer sustain your own life as you have known it—your kids will be willing to take your hand as you move along toward the end of your run on earth.

Those future days will reveal whether a mom will have "her children rise up and call her blessed," or if a dad fits the description, "the father of a righteous man has great joy." If "parents are the pride of their children," as Proverbs describes it, moms, dads, and kids will end their run together with mutual interdependence, loving it to their final day this side of heaven.

8

You *Can* Take It with You

Finding Freedom from Unsolvable Problems

It's ironic that in our culture everyone's biggest complaint
is about not having enough time; yet nothing terrifies us
more than the thought of eternity.[1]

Dennis Miller

It is a fairly typical week in our household. One son has a new
girlfriend, one son just had his break up with him, the other is
still a couple of weeks into recovery from breaking up with his,
Mark has a new job and Phil needs more hours at his, applica-
tions for college are in process, a father/son trip is scheduled
for this weekend, guitar lessons happened Monday, vacation
plans got decided for next month, we are preparing for fifteen
guests at a holiday party, we RSVP for a work celebration today,
a youth retreat just finished, I got a haircut last night, Lynn has
a routine medical test tomorrow, bills have to get paid, one of
the kids is a little ill, there is a math test at school, a class project
is due tomorrow, Tim is working on a take-home test, we go
for driver's licensing later, two members of our extended fam-

ily are facing relational breakdowns, my sister starts radiation treatment for breast cancer, a friend just found a lump in her breast, I had a business trip, I am working on this book, email keeps coming to all five of us, instant messaging keeps popping up, one of eight phones (each person's cell, plus our home phone, home fax, and "kid line") rings at all hours, someone left the TV on, the music is playing too loud, the garage door was left open, I melted when one of the boys hugged their mom, I cringed when one of them ridiculed her, I confronted another instance of blatant disrespect, the computer crashed and got fixed, a rush to the bank covered the real estate tax bill just in time, we grocery shopped twice so we could find the bargains at Costco, we managed to squeeze in a workout last night, church is tonight if we make it, yard work should be done, cars should be washed, gutters should be cleaned, laundry has been done, dry cleaning dropped off and picked up, we attend a farewell to longtime friends on Friday afternoon but don't want to face the sad good-bye, Tim has a small-group social outing later this week, Lynn's best friend's birthday was celebrated over lunch yesterday about the time my best friend called for prayer, there is a niece's birthday this week, one of the boys needs a gift for a party he's invited to, and there is an extra class to attend at church on Saturday. And it is only Wednesday!

It's no wonder an A, B, C, D, E, F, G approach to parenting does not automatically churn out great kids. If your life is anything like ours—and if you tally a typical week's activities it may make ours look leisurely—reality will conspire to undermine the formulas and automatic answers. Whenever you hear someone offer simplistic, one-size-fits-all child-rearing tips, do not feel bad about your natural suspicions. Wait long enough and you will see it. Parents who limit themselves to the A–G approach will have children take them on a roller coaster ride that their recipes and prescriptions cannot explain.

Why? Because that is the nature of life. The general principles, methods, and procedures help, to be sure, but their power is in *how you apply them*.

178

Staying above the Fray

This book has included some parenting basics because you do have to know some fundamentals to be good at it. As I mentioned at the beginning, understanding the "A through G" of parenting—and then some—matters. Every parent needs to know some basics on child development, authority, education, spiritual direction, money management, and navigating the teenage years. Nothing you've read in this book is contrary to the fundamentals of good parenting.

As a parent, your job is to, in some sense, stay above the fray so you can remain responsive to situations as they develop. You cannot reduce the adventure of parenting to drawing dot-to-dot, painting by the numbers. Your children are works of art whose complexities will never be that simplified. Like a great artist, the ideas at your disposal will be your color palette, but you will need to apply them deftly to create the hues and touches that come together in a masterpiece.

Your artistry should increase now that you have seen your craft through the lenses of polarity management. You can understand and bear the tension you feel because you now see the picture in a different light. You understand the goals you are trying to achieve in your kids' lives over the long haul. Brought together, they look like this:

Challenge to Meet	Tightrope to Walk	Goal to Achieve
Training	Limits—Freedom	Wise Decision Making
Discipline	Punishment—Nurture	Self-Discipline
Spiritual	Tradition—Choice	Personal Faith
Adolescent	Tender Love—Tough Love	Minimal Wounds
Financial	Support—Self-Sufficiency	Economic Independence
Interdependence	Attachment—Autonomy	Long-Term Relationship

179

These are not a one-size-fits-all set of goals, though. How they materialize in each son or daughter will only become clear over time. Your child's wisdom in decisions, self-discipline, and personal faith will differ greatly from that of other children. The wounds they suffer, especially in adolescence, will trigger growth unique to them. How they achieve economic independence and what shape your lifelong relationship takes will evolve over many years of your joint journey.

A Look in the Mirror

Now that you have the comprehensive picture in mind, I want you to bring together all you're thinking from the previous chapters. You can start by honestly assessing your family, your parenting.

Once you have read the chapters, you are ready to review your status and opportunities. Reflect on the chart above, asking yourself, "Where am I on each tightrope? Where do I tend to land on each tightrope? How well am I meeting each challenge, really? What am I doing to accomplish each goal?" You might choose to work through the exercises in the leader's guide. Small groups studying this together can provide invaluable input. For maximum objectivity, ask friends and family how they see your situation.

After you have taken some time to reflect, it is time to make your assessment tangible. Mark an X on each continuum below. Ask your spouse, and even your kids, for their opinion if you are doing this together. You could even use different colors to chart each person's perceptions, discovering where you agree, and talking through your differences of opinion. Just like there are no right answers to most of your parenting dilemmas, there is little black and white in the process of compiling your learning. You may even sense some shifts since you started reading.

	The training challenge:	
Limits	————————————————	Freedom

	The discipline challenge:	
Punishment	————————————————	Nurture

	The spiritual challenge:	
Tradition	————————————————	Choice

	The adolescent challenge:	
Tender Love	————————————————	Tough Love

	The financial challenge:	
Support	————————————————	Self-Sufficiency

	The interdependence challenge:	
Attachment	————————————————	Autonomy

If you felt a little frustration over one or two of the marks you had to make, do not hold on to it for long. Likewise, whenever you felt pride, rest assured that it will have a short shelf life—just around the bend something will knock you off balance.

When I chart my current course, I feel a sense of relief on the one hand and resolve on the other. I'm relieved because the tension inherent in parenting makes sense all over again. Resolve comes from seeing where I currently tilt too far on any one continuum, a clue I need to do *both* good things.

Where are you right now? Can you reflect on times in your life as a mom or dad when you've been keeping both ends of a particular continuum in better tension? As you compare notes with other parents, who is doing a little better at the moment to keep things in balance?

Like an engine, one of these sets of tensions may be just a little out of tune; simple awareness is enough to deal with temporary misfiring. However, you may realize there is a piston about ready to break, so you need to do a little repair work. Regardless, do not be discouraged by it. You are facing parenting reality, where both parents and children often prove remarkable resilience, especially when they can spot an issue that must be faced.

Customizing Your Approach

Once you have marked each continuum, it is time to determine your next steps. What specific actions can you take to live in the tension, honoring both ends of each continuum? Which tightropes require the most attention? How might they vary with each child? In two-parent households, where do you need more conversation to be united and consistent? When might more discussion with your children enhance your planning? You may want to seek clarification by reviewing prior chapters as you work through the leader's guide exercises.

You may not have all the answers you would like right away because you need to keep moving forward, searching for answers by watching yourself, your kids, or your family with newfound awareness. Fight off the temptation to seek right answers or quick formulas. Remember, the reason there is tension is because you have to achieve two competing good things.

Thoroughly answering these questions and choosing specific actions can be such a big job you'll not know where to start. So try shortening the time line. What area(s) needs the most attention over the next ninety days? Of the action steps you identified, what is most readily pursued tomorrow? What will give the most return for the effort? How might you focus more energy there?

In other words, you probably cannot do everything at once. You will have to pick and choose, decide on a sequence of actions, or tailor different next steps for each child. Don't let feelings of being overwhelmed paralyze you. You are likely to be experimenting anyway, so your initial steps may not be the full change you need to consider. By moving forward you will learn more along the way, and can keep comparing notes with others, monitoring how a child responds, and staying balanced on the tightrope as you continue walking ahead.

Break down key insights and changes into individual activities; this can really help. You may want to assess each parent's contribution to the family's potential progress and the extent you can involve a daughter or son in some tangible way. You could focus on specific tasks, actions, scheduling issues, or ways you will kindly cue each other when imbalance reappears. You might even want each family member to ask, "Where is my heart on this issue? Where do I need to grow?" At each point, though, keep moving from the specific to the more general chart of challenges, tightropes, and goals so you do not lose the big picture.

Doing this kind of assessment, and formulating next steps to correct imbalance, is not a one-time activity. Nothing changes more quickly than kids, and your ongoing growth will affect how you shape your future together. So from time to time you will need to take a fresh snapshot of where you are with each of these areas, making sure you are keeping the tension settings in tune.

There will also be some moments when you feel like child rearing could not be going worse. But rather than pile on guilt for what you allegedly missed in Parenting 101, you will suddenly realize how your feelings connect to the parenting tightrope.

When parents openly and honestly face the six challenges, walking the tightrope together, family life becomes an enjoyable adventure. You are not reactive, but proactive. Your time together changes texture due to your increased intentionality. Momentum builds, despite the ups and downs along the way. You more readily diagnose blockages to connecting with your kids, so you can develop a sense of deepening relationship. From time to time, mom and dad move from opposing each other over their shared challenge; because they understand the tension underlying their points of view, they can experience true camaraderie.

But this does not happen automatically. Mere discussion and understanding will not move parents and families forward. It requires your ongoing initiative. It always takes action: being bold enough to walk the tightrope no matter what tension arises.

A New Freedom

When parents and children stop trying to solve unsolvable problems and instead enter into the tensions every family faces, authenticity rises. Nobody has to pretend there are right answers to which they have the inside scoop. A family becomes more natural, more real, more normal, and free from the need to act like all is well when it isn't. As such a family begins to touch other families, they are in turn changed—one child, one parent, one family at a time. Instead of feeling guilty about not reaching unrealistic standards of parenting, moms and dads can lean into the Holy Spirit for guidance.

The change is not just in the look and feel of a family, though. Children begin to change, along with their parents. They have a shot at moving toward the goals you dream of for them:

- **Wise Decision Making**—Children exercise increasing freedom within limits they choose for themselves.
- **Self-Discipline**—They know when to feel appropriate guilt because they are safe enough to admit wrong.
- **Personal Faith**—Their spiritual path becomes their choice, having the framework of a family's faith story.
- **Minimal Wounds**—Teenagers stop short of drastic choices with long-term damages to them and others.

- **Economic Independence**—There is a gradual weaning process to shift their support responsibilities; mom and dad are a safety net rather than a supplier.
- **Long-Term Relationship**—Newfound interdependence triggers relational growth for a lifetime.

When parents understand that rigid child-rearing models and practices no longer bind them, they are indeed free. Free to fail; free to experiment; free to become open about struggles. Children will not be upset or surprised by confusion and clarity, chaos and control, laughter and tears—all in the same evening!

But to get to all six goals without compromising the quality of your parenting you must stare fearlessly into the reality of these tensions. Ironic, isn't it? By adopting this way of thinking—being OK with not knowing for sure the right answer, getting used to tension—you find freedom from tension.

You were never going to be rid of the tension between multiple sets of polarities anyway. At least now you can be liberated from feeling like you missed out on parenting done "right." Delight in the process more than the supposed mistakes, keep focused on the goals, on the artistic side of crafting a kid's soul, and you suddenly resolve much of the tension all of us feel in being the best moms and dads we can.

As important as it is to continue to drink in new parenting ideas—but just as ideas, not formulas, magic solutions, or instant recipes for success—nothing will displace an underlying truth: effectively growing up kids is no dot-to-dot drawing process where, if you follow the right sequence and draw straight lines, you'll get a true picture. You can settle for the false security of matching up to someone else's blueprint for coloring-book-level drafting. That is not parenting, though.

Parenting requires engagement and achievement at a higher level, the daring you see in acrobatics, where you must balance, stay cool despite spectator reaction, and concentrate more on the tightrope than on the results of a fall. Growing in the skills of tightrope walking will get you through all the challenges of parenting—by managing dynamic tensions that stretch you at every turn.

No Greater Challenge . . . or Reward

Parenting is one of the greatest tests we will ever know, but it is also one of our greatest opportunities. Remember the Bible's description in Proverbs 17:6? "Children's children are a crown to the aged." It may sometimes feel like a weighty crown to wear, once in a while becoming like a crown of thorns.

Every now and then, you can figuratively dismount the tightrope and, from the perspective of a firm floor, look up and can think, "Wow, I did that?!?" Your sense of relief and exhilaration as you relive the harrowing moments, thrilling achievements, and fulfilling effort will help you realize what a privilege you had to take such a remarkable journey.

When you see the legacy of your life in the lives of the people you invested in the most—your own kids—there are few things that could be more of a crowning achievement. It is challenging, for sure. But if you walk with wisdom, and lean into God's principles, into his church, into each other, you will find one of the greatest payoffs in your lives.

There is only one thing that passes from this life to the next: people. Everything else fades in comparison to that single investment. What you deposit into the lives of those closest to you does live on, sometimes for generations, often rippling into the lives your children touch. You can make no more profound choice than to embark on whatever is left in your parenting journey with all you have. The payoff is for all of eternity.

Leader's Guide for
Small Group Interactions

These group exercises are designed to help you identify parenting tightrope tensions and team up with other group members to walk through the various challenges presented by each tension. It is important for leaders to read each chapter first and then prepare to complete the corresponding activities.

Ideally, each member would have a copy of the book so you can work through all these tensions after having read the material. Since some people may not get through the reading before a specific meeting, you should be prepared to provide a brief overview of the main points of the chapter so the group can interact with the ideas well.

Each of the eight exercises, one for each chapter in the book, is designed to maximize participation and help members engage with the content of the chapter in ways that build community. Each lesson includes instructions on the following:

Overview—a description of the meeting time, including:

Purpose of the chapter
Purpose of the lesson

Meeting preparation—specific instructions for the group leader to help lead the time a group has together:

Scripture
Time required for interaction
Materials needed
Activity to complete

Walking the tightrope—a group activity or interaction that guides members to identify the tension in family of origin and/or present family.

Focus on interactive, experiential learning and discussion. It may take more than one meeting to process the material for each of the six tensions parents face—but it does not have to. You can set your own pace; time guidelines are included to give you an idea of what an average group of 8–10 people might be able to accomplish during a meeting.

Since there are usually more activities and material to be covered than most groups will complete in one session, you will have to pick and choose from time to time, depending on how intensely you tackle each chapter. You may decide to spread a study over more than one meeting, as well. *If you can plan ahead, consider a small group retreat, timed to coincide with the study of chapter 3.*

A normal meeting will include other elements, such as serving tasks in which the group is involved, prayer, times for celebration and affirmation, Scripture reading, worship, food (the highlight of many meetings!), and so on. Since you know your group better than anyone, you can tailor each lesson to best meet its needs.

A couple of additional caveats:

- Some families are dealing with troubled children, who may even need medical help, so be prepared for those delicate moments of realization.

188

- The activities will usually be appropriate for both single parents and couples, but you may have to choose how to use some of the material.

Just as parents walk a tightrope, small group leaders manage tension in most of the gatherings they host. When you feel that tension, it probably indicates you are maintaining the balance your group needs!

Chapter 1
Welcome to the
Parenting Tightrope

OVERVIEW

Purpose of the chapter: To understand the concept of polarity management in relationship to parenting.

Purpose of the lesson: To recognize tensions in your own family.

MEETING PREPARATION

- Read chapter 1.
- Be prepared to recap the key issues of the chapter for group members who did not do the reading.
- Understand the tension between two good things: Polarity Management.
- Understand the difference between *how* you think about your parenting challenge and *what* you think about your parenting challenge (see page 34).

Scripture

Proverbs 17:6

Time required

45–60 minutes

Materials needed

Each couple/person brings a picture of their children
Whiteboard or large sheets of paper for brainstorming
Markers

Activities to complete

Discuss reactions to Proverbs 17:6.

Show pictures of children and describe one tension you face with each of them.

Brainstorm the tensions you currently feel as you attempt to raise your children.

WALKING THE TIGHTROPE

Discussion

(3 min. per member) Proverbs 17:6 says "Children's children are a crown to the aged, and parents are the pride of their children." What is your initial reaction to this proverb? If you look at your family of origin, can you identify a positive aspect to your relationship with your parents or grandparents? Are they proud of you? Are you proud of them? Why or why not?

Show and tell

(3 min. per member) Display the pictures of each of your children and tell one tension you are facing with them in child rearing. Do not try to "fix" the tension for each other at this point, just recognize it.

Brainstorm

List possible tensions you have faced as a child and now as a parent. Remember in brainstorming you are only listing the thought with minimal conversation. Each idea is valid. After you have completed an initial round of brainstorming, spend some time determining which of the tensions are really two good things you must do as a parent, which stand in opposition to each other.

Conclusion

The tensions you listed are real. As you learned from the first chapter, some of them are present because there are so many good things you must do as a parent. Acknowledging this reality is the beginning of understanding a new way to look at child rearing. *How* you think about your parenting challenges may carry you further than *what* you think as you walk these tightropes.

Prayer

If each small group member is comfortable praying, it would be good to have them each commit to the upcoming studies by saying out loud a prayer similar to this:

Father, I pray you will open my eyes to new ways of looking at my parenting. Help me to be willing to learn some new ideas that may be outside of my comfort zone right now. Amen.

Chapter 2
What Part of "No" Don't You Understand?

OVERVIEW

Purpose of the chapter: To develop wise decision-making abilities in children.

Purpose of the lesson: To learn when and how to apply the parenting skills of modeling, instructing, coaching, correcting, and embedding.

MEETING PREPARATION

- Read chapter 2.
- Be prepared to recap the key issues of the chapter for group members who did not do the reading.
- Know the difference between modeling, instructing, coaching, correcting, and embedding.

Scripture

1 Corinthians 2:16; 1 Corinthians 10:23–32; Proverbs 22:6

Time required

60–75 minutes

Materials needed

Whiteboard or large sheets of paper

Markers

Activities to complete

Discuss parental modeling.

Understand the various aspects of training.

WALKING THE TIGHTROPE

Discussion

(3 min. per member) The chapter discussed one set of parents' love of motorcycling and how they are modeling riding for kids who now want motorcycles of their own. What is something you model that could make you swallow hard if your children were to participate in the activity?

"Best practices" study

(45 min.) Write the different training activities across the top of your board or a large sheet of paper, such as this:

Model, instruct, coach, correct, embed

Have each couple or individual parent share one positive way they currently engage in each of these activities. The ideas they describe will help other parents learn some of the ways they can grow. Such "best practices" will not always be well received by everyone, and you can gauge your group's authenticity by how they interact over the methods they employ as parents. But as people share, the discussion will spark learning about the differences between the various approaches to training, and appreciation for the good ideas other parents employ to train their children. Not everyone will have examples for each area, which will help them realize where they can develop in their ability to walk the training tightrope. Some of the discussion may lead to some joint problem solving over ways to handle various situations.

Conclusion

Proverbs 22:6 says, "Train a child in the way he should go, and when he is old he will not turn from it." Our role as parents is to help our children understand the paths they need to walk, which will take a variety of methods, employed by all of us as good students of our children as we lead them.

Prayer

Break into pairs and pray for each other, that (a) you would be willing to stop doing one thing you do not want to pass on to your children, and (b) you will each start doing one life-giving activity you want to pass on to your children.

Chapter 3
Living with the Law of Big

OVERVIEW

Purpose of the chapter: To help children develop self-discipline.

Purpose of the lesson: To discover parent's and children's temperaments, so parents can apply various methods of discipline in both an age and temperament appropriate manner.

MEETING PREPARATION

- Read chapter 3.
- Be prepared to recap the key issues of the chapter for group members who did not do the reading.
- Be familiar with the Myers-Briggs Temperament Type Indicator.
- Be ready to discuss the differing temperaments of couples and children.
- Be ready to field questions or be a buffer for strong opinions about spanking or other physical displays of discipline.

Scripture

Proverbs 19:18; Proverbs 22:15; Proverbs 23:13; Ephesians 6:4; 1 Corinthians 13:1

Time required

(65 min.) This chapter has a greater than normal amount of information, which may make it challenging to digest and apply it all in one session. You may want to slow the pace of work and discussion and cover this lesson in two or more meetings. One other idea: take your small group away on an overnight retreat and structure multiple discussion times to uncover and apply the lessons from this chapter.

Materials needed

Whiteboard or large sheet of paper
Markers
Note cards—2 per member—and pens

Four questions

1. When interacting with people, do you get more energized by being with lots of people in a room (Extraversion) or quiet conversation escapes with one or two friends (Introversion)?
2. Do you tend to think about things by relying on your instincts or hunches (iNtuition) or by using evidence and data—and the more the better (Sensation)?
3. Are your decisions based on dispassionate processing in your head (Thinking) or following your heart, empathy, and emotional pull (Feeling)?
4. Do you settle things by driving for closure (Judgment) or staying open and fluid (Perception)?
   (You may want to obtain a copy of Tieger and Tieger, *Do What You Are*, or Keirsey and Bates, *Please Understand Me: Character and Temperament Types* for reference.)

Activities to complete

Each member assesses their temperament.

Each member assesses their children's temperament.
Determine how each member's children learn.
Identify character traits to develop with discipline.
Brainstorm possible misbehavior and options for discipline.

WALKING THE TIGHTROPE

Have copies of the four questions listed above available for each person to look at. Each member must do their own assessment.

On your own

(5 min.) Find a quiet spot and work on the assessment to determine what your temperament combination is.

Pair with spouse or other group member

(10 min.) 1. Talk about how you see yourself—not how you wish you were, but how and who you really are in the four dimensions of temperament. Affirm each others' perceptions, or identify where your opinions differ.

2. Discuss how your differences manifest themselves in your relationships and family. Since God made you to be unique and your temperament will not change, one of the best things you can do is to be aware of your tendencies and moderate them out of love for others.

Group debrief

(10 min.) Bring the group back together, and have each person share their temperament type combination. Open up the discussion to allow group members to affirm the descriptions and make observations about their understanding or surprise about a person's conclusions. Be aware of group dynamics; there will be expanded insight between members about each

other and some room for disagreement. Allow the discussion to lead the learning.

Pair with spouse or other group member

(10 min.) Along with your spouse or a friend, do an assessment of your children. If children are still infants or toddlers, you will only be able to form preliminary opinions about them.

Use this time to determine how your child learns—by pain, observation, or intuition—as well. (See pages 68–69.)

Group debrief

(10 min.) Bring the group back together again, and have each person or couple share the temperament type combination for each child. Allow group members to affirm the descriptions, and bring some objective observations about each other's children, to the extent they can. There may be some difference of opinion, but that is all right, because that will lead to further learning about both parents and children. Discussion will do some of the teaching once again.

Brainstorm

(5 min.) Brainstorm a list of character traits that you would like to see developed in your children. You can start with the Bible, for example Galatians 5:22–23, but expand it to include other moral or ethical traits. Remember the rules of healthy brainstorming (chapter 1's lesson). Once you have completed an initial list, narrow it down to the top dozen or so traits the group would agree are needed in their children.

Discussion

(15 min.) Proverbs 19:18; 22:15; and 23:13 contain words of wisdom concerning the sinful bent children have, and the need for parents to help them learn to curb their actions and/or attitudes. On the whiteboard or large sheet of paper make

two columns. In the first column, list common misbehaviors of children. In the second column, list possible discipline methods. Try to think outside of the box in listing methods. Discuss how temperament differences might make it wise to implement them according to the temperament of you and your children. What do you need to let go of to let your child be who he or she is, and where do you need to step in?

CONCLUSION

The discipline challenge is more than just saying yes or no to your children. It is about understanding who you and your children are— by temperament, learning style, and character needs—so that you can punish more wisely and nurture more effectively.

PRAYER

As you close out this extended time together, thank God for making each of you so incredible and unique. Ask that he will give you wisdom to know where to moderate your temperament, to share the parenting between spouses, and to let your child learn—sometimes the hard way.

Chapter 4
Don't Tell Me *That* Old, Old Story

OVERVIEW

Purpose of the chapter: To help children take ownership of their faith.

Purpose of the lesson: To identify how each member of your family connects with God; to take steps towards developing each person's spiritual pathway.

MEETING PREPARATION

- Read chapter 4.
- Be prepared to recap the key issues of the chapter for group members who did not do the reading.

Scripture

Genesis 4:1–16; Deuteronomy 4:9; 6:6–9; Esther 14:14; 2 Timothy 1:5; Luke 15:11–32

Time required

55–75 minutes

Materials needed

Copies of the Spiritual Pathways list (page 89–90)
Note cards and pens

Activities to complete

Discuss various spiritual pathways and identify each member and child's preferred path.

Identify each member and child's spiritual gifts.

WALKING THE TIGHTROPE

Discussion

(2 min. per member) The chapter describes how important partners are to the success of any venture (pages 87–88). Who are you partnering with for the sake of your child's spiritual growth?

(1 min. per member) If you could expand your partners, who would you ask to join you in this partnership? Could you do that this week? What will you say to invite them into this process with you?

(20 min.) Each group member should have the list of nine sacred pathways Gary Thomas describes for how people can connect with God. On the note cards, identify the areas that do not spark an interest in you. Out of those that remain, highlight the one or two that you find yourself returning to in your spiritual walk. Of those you have not experienced, is there one that you would like to try? Once you have finalized some thinking about yourself, review the list to sort out the spiritual pathways you see in your children. How might you facilitate ones they seem attracted to, or experiment with those they haven't tried?

(20 min.) Read the lists of spiritual gifts from Romans 12:6–8, 1 Corinthians 12:7–11, and Ephesians 4:11. Go through the same process with note cards as you review them, identifying those descriptions that spark little interest, and highlighting the one or two you tend to demonstrate. Again, go through the same process for your children.

CONCLUSION

You have a unique pathway to walking with God, and so do your kids. Each of your spiritual gifts marks you, as well. It is a clue about the vastness of God's creativity and how creative you might need to be in parenting your children toward connecting with him. Lean into the partners around you, and you will walk the spiritual tightrope well!

PRAYER

Read Psalm 107:21; pray prayers of thanksgiving for God's unfailing love.

Chapter 5
Are You Sure You Want to Die on That Hill?

OVERVIEW

Purpose of the chapter: To get kids through adolescence with minimal wounds.

Purpose of the lesson: To learn some new ways to stand strong in the face of adversity with your children.

MEETING PREPARATION

- Read chapter 5.
- Be prepared to recap the key issues of the chapter for group members who did not do the reading.
- Assess your group's current, emerging, and potential parenting issues during adolescence.
- Choose the discussion questions and the form your prayer time will take.

Scripture

Galatians 6:1; Hebrews 12:5–6

Time required

60–80 minutes (including potential expanded prayer time)

Materials needed

A good imagination

Activities to complete

Selected activities and prayer options.
Discussions of tough love and unconditional love scenarios.
Role-play parent and child situations.

WALKING THE TIGHTROPE

Discussion

(5 min. per member) Each member chooses one of the following questions to answer:

The chapter summarized eleven different areas of training that could require either tough love or unconditional love: work, jobs, schedules, planning, grades, friends, mistakes, transportation, arrests, authority, and girl/boyfriends.

Choose one of these categories and describe how you dealt with it when you were an adolescent. How do you wish it would have been handled? What was the outcome from your point of view?

OR

Describe a present-day situation either where you are rescuing one of your children or where you are giving tough love. What is your child's response?

Role-play

(5 min. per situation) This role-play activity is designed to give parents an opportunity to practice the three keys—clear expectations, clear warnings, and clear consequences. It will help both parents and children understand how important it is to be clear in expectations.

One group member will play the parent and one the child. Following the role-play evaluate whether the three keys were used by the parent. What could have been improved on?

Role-play #1: The child has just come home after curfew. He or she was the driver. A parent meets the child at the door—role-play the ensuing conflict.

Role-play #2: The parent has just turned the corner into a child's bedroom. The child is summoned to the disaster zone they failed to clean up yesterday. Role-play the next part of the conversation.

Role-play #3: A neighbor just disclosed to the parent how the child was observed _____ (fill in age-relevant misbehavior). The parent calls the child into the kitchen for a confrontation. Role-play the dialogue that follows.

Discussion

(10 min.) Read Galatians 6:1. Where and how can the group give its members help in creating a more restorative community? Are there times and ways the group might come together around its children? In what ways might you provide each other safe places to go with frustrations and relief, giving each other strength to carry this burden? If there is tension between one parent and a child, how could the other parent move into the primary parenting role for a season?

CONCLUSION

This tension is one of those that could have heightened intensity for one or more families in the group right now. Your group can help them hang on for the wildest part of the ride and provide wisdom for wrestling with the tension between tender and tough love. As you navigate when to be more hands-off, explicit, flexible, constructive, and collaborative, remain hopeful and prayerful about getting through this season with minimal long-term wounds.

PRAYER

(10 min.) Pair off and pray for specific instances where you need wisdom to stay on the tightrope between tender love and tough love. Pray that you each have courage to be tough when you want to rescue your children unwisely.

ALTERNATE PRAYER

If there are parents facing some hard times with older children, and you sense that they and their children need focused prayer, have the group physically surround them and pray for the particular situation(s) they face. Repeat the exercise with other parents who need to be covered by the group's prayers.

Chapter 6
Be All That You Can Be

OVERVIEW

Purpose of the chapter: To help children achieve financial independence.

Purpose of the lesson: To begin a budget for your children in the short term and identify careers that might be good for them in the long term.

MEETING PREPARATION

- Read chapter 6.
- Be prepared to recap the key issues of the chapter for group members who did not do the reading.
- Determine the discussion track you want to take, if you cannot cover the whole chapter.
- If you choose to have the discussion about college funding or other issues, and want a financial planner to join you, make those arrangements.
- If you choose to work on budgets for the children, have information ready to guide your group through this exercise.

Scripture

Psalm 139:13–14; Mark 4:18–19; Romans 12:6; 1 Timothy 5:8; 2 Thessalonians 3:10

Time required

75–90 minutes (Due to the two parts of this chapter, you may want to devote two sessions to it and slow the pace of your activity to 60 minutes for each meeting.)

Materials needed

Whiteboard or large sheet of paper
Markers
Graph paper to work on budgets

Activities to complete (choose from below)

Discussion around lifestyle choices and spending.
Setting up a budget for your children.
Conversation on preparing for college funding.
Discussion of job experiences leading to children's careers.

WALKING THE TIGHTROPE

Discussion

(3 min. per member) What is your reaction to this statement? "Find what you love to do, and you'll never have to work."

Discussion

(3 min. per member) Describe what has determined your lifestyle. Is it parents, friends, society, or something else? Are you satisfied with your choice? How does your spending define your "points of insanity"?

Budget preparation

(40 min.) Write on the whiteboard or large sheet of paper budget areas children can control, such as wardrobe, enter-

tainment, spending, giving, haircuts, school supplies, school lunches, and gifts. Include items that are a part of your budget or spending. How much money does a child need at various ages for each category?

Transfer the categories to the graph paper and create a column for each year of your children's life, beginning with the current age of the youngest child. How would you allocate current and future spending to each budget until a child achieves financial independence by age 16 to 18?

Alternate discussion

(30 min.) What are your educational expectations? What is your educational background? Based on those, how will you approach college funding? Consider having a financial planner come in to talk about possibilities and needs for parents who want to begin planning for it.

Alternate discussion

(5 min. per member) What jobs did you hold in high school and college? Can you identify something you learned from each of your jobs? How did these jobs clarify what you would be doing for a career? What might your children learn from varied jobs you could encourage them to consider?

Alternate discussion

(5 min. per member) Refer to the chapter on spiritual gifts: How could the spiritual gifts of each of your children fit into a career?

Refer to the work you did on temperaments: What career fields would be good for your children to explore? Can you begin to see who your children are and are not? Are you okay with that?

Conclusion

The work of planning for the future is just that: work. It takes initiative on your part to engage the right process and people in discussion. It also takes preparation to guide your children into the reality of life outside your "nest." Although it can feel frightening, look into the future and wonder how your children will do. God has made a promise to you and your kids, "'Never will I leave you; never will I forsake you.' So we say with confidence, 'The Lord is my helper; I will not be afraid.'" (Heb. 13:5–6).

Prayer

Close your time with the leader praying a general prayer of wisdom for the future direction of each of your group members and their children.

Chapter 7
Umbilical Cords, Apron Strings, and Phone Lines

Overview

Purpose of the chapter: To build the foundation for healthy long-term relationships between adult children and their parents.

Purpose of the lesson: To identify areas you need to become autonomous as an adult child with your parents and ways you can help your children walk the tightrope of attachment *and* autonomy.

Meeting Preparation

- Read chapter 7
- Be prepared to recap the key issues of the chapter for group members who did not do the reading.
- Identify the time line you want to have your members diagram.

Scripture

Proverbs 17:6; Proverbs 23:24; Proverbs 31:28

Time required

60–90 minutes (You may want to assign the time line ahead of the meeting to increase the time you can devote to discussing them.)

Materials needed

A roll of craft paper or larger paper sheets to draw out a time line

Pens or markers

Activities to complete

Due to the many different combinations of parent/child ages and stages of life, choose the activities that accommodate the possibilities represented in your group. In the end, each small group member will draw a time line showing where autonomy was encouraged or discouraged in their own lives.

WALKING THE TIGHTROPE

Time line—choice 1

Draw a time line from birth to the present for you, the parent. Indicate times or ages where you were allowed autonomy and/or where you tried to be autonomous and were held back.

Discussion

(10 min. per member) Describe the significant events you charted on your time line. Answer these questions:

What were the circumstances around the event?

How did you feel during and after the experience?

What would you have liked to change about the experience?

214

Optional follow-up discussion

Are there some unhealthy relating patterns between you and
your parents that you need to face? What are they?

Where do you need to either make a break with your parents
or reenter a healthy relating pattern with your parents?

How will you do this? List some of the steps needed to
grow in autonomy.

Time line—choice 2

Draw a time line of your own child's life. Indicate the points
in their lives when they have tried to be autonomous, or perhaps
when they have not taken enough initiative to make the break
with you and you have had to push them "out of the nest" a bit.

Discussion

(10 min. per member) Describe the significant events you
charted on your child's time line. Answer these questions:

What were the circumstances around the event you chose
to highlight?

How did your child handle the greater independence?

How did you handle letting your child be more independent?

What could you do better or differently the next time your
child indicates (s)he wants greater freedom?

Where can you give up control when everything inside of
you is wanting to hold on too long?

What rites of passage can you incorporate into your children's
lives to help them recognize that greater autonomy is expected and celebrated?

Final Discussion

(10 min.) *For couples*—What are you building into your marriage so it will be strong when you no longer have the children
and their needs to be the center of your daily conversation?

215

For single parents—What are you doing to be ready for an empty nest? What skills, hobbies, and friendships are you developing so that you will be ready?

CONCLUSION

We have been taught to be highly involved with our kids and their activities. As they grow older those apron strings need to be loosened . . . and eventually cut. As parents and children grow into the people God wants them to be, the relating patterns mature into that of adult peers. But the road to that point can be a rocky one. Don't give up—cheer each other on!

PRAYER IF YOU CHOSE ACTIVITY 1

Ask forgiveness for residual anger that may be blocking a healthy relationship with your parents.

Pray for each other to have wisdom to know how to enter into a healthy relationship with your parents.

PRAYER IF YOU CHOSE ACTIVITY 2

Pair off by couple or single parent units.

Ask forgiveness for being too controlling and not helping your children grow up.

Pray for each other to have the courage to let go.

And finally, pray that your love will grow deeper as your children grow older and grow away from you.

Chapter 8
You *Can* Take It with You

OVERVIEW

Purpose of the chapter: To bring all the learning from chapters 2–7 together for overall assessment.

Purpose of the lesson: To create tangible next steps for each family, so they can choose the tightrope lesson to work on that will make the greatest difference in their parenting.

MEETING PREPARATION

- Read chapter 8.
- Be prepared to recap the key issues of the chapter for group members who did not do the reading.

Scripture

Proverbs 17:6

Time required

60–70 minutes

Materials needed

A copy of the chart on page 179 listing the six tightropes
Pens for each member

Activities to complete

Identify where each member is on each of the six tightropes.
Discuss next steps for each member on one tightrope.

WALKING THE TIGHTROPE

Tightrope assessment

(5 min.) Use the chart listing the six tightropes and mark
where you are in the process of balancing each tightrope. To
make things interesting you can make two marks—one where
you were when you started this book and the second one
indicating where you are today.

Discussion

(5 min. per member) Ask your spouse or other group members if your assessment is accurate, through their observations.
You may want to choose one or more of the tightropes to talk
about at further length.

Additional assessment

(10 min.) Once you have marked each continuum, determine at least one next step you need to take for each one.

Discussion

(5 min. per member) What specific actions can you take
to help live in the tension, honoring both ends of each continuum? Which tightropes require most attention? How might
they vary with each child?

Conclusion

Parenting is a consuming experience—for life. It takes conscious effort and initiative. Recognize the tightropes and where you are on each of them. Keep striving to recover your balance whenever the adventure of child-rearing challenges your sense of equilibrium. And never, never, never give up!

Prayer

Use this last lesson to offer prayers of celebration for the next steps you will each be taking as you learn to balance on the tightropes.

Notes

Chapter 1: Welcome to the Parenting Tightrope

1. Martin Mull, ThinkExist.com, Copyright ThinkExist 1999–2004, http://en.thinkexist.com/quotes/Martin_Mull/.

2. Marvin Hamlisch and Alan Bergman, "The Way We Were" (New York: Colgems Music Corp., 1973).

3. This is not an actual title. Nobody has been bold enough to write a book bearing that title yet, so don't rush out to look for it even if you, like me, wish someone would do so.

4. Barry Johnson, *Polarity Management: Identifying and Managing Unsolvable Problems* (Amherst, MA: HRD Press, 1992, 1996). Polarity Management™ is a trademark of Polarity Management Associates, LLC.

5. For more on this, see Bill Donahue and Russ Robinson, *Walking the Small Group Tightrope* (Grand Rapids: Zondervan, 2003).

Chapter 2: What Part of "No" Don't You Understand?

1. Jerry Seinfeld, *Jerry Seinfeld Live on Broadway: I'm Telling You for the Last Time,* DVD, directed by Marty Callner (HBO Studios, 1998).

2. See Genesis 2:8–18.

3. Galatians 5:1

4. John 8:36

5. 1 Corinthians 2:16

6. Galatians 5:25

7. Galatians 5:13

8. 1 Corinthians 10:23–32

9. Dr. Henry Cloud and Dr. John Townsend, *Boundaries with Kids* (Grand Rapids: Zondervan, 1998), 40.

Chapter 3: Living with the Law of Big

1. Bill Cosby, Copyright 2004 BrainyMedia.com, property of Xplore, Inc., http://www.brainyquote.com/quotes/authors/b/bill_cosby.html.

221

2. Ken Davis, *Lighten Up* (Grand Rapids: Zondervan, 2000), 152–53.

3. Ephesians 6:4 TLB

4. 1 Corinthians 13:1

5. David Keirsey and Marilyn Bates, *Please Understand Me: Character and Temperament Types* (Del Mar, CA: Prometheus, 1984).

6. Paul D. Tieger and Barbara Barron-Tieger, *Nurture by Nature* (Boston: Little, Brown, 1997).

7. I heard McManus's thoughts expressed in an informal teaching setting. For further principles on character development, see Erwin Raphael McManus, *Uprising, A Revolution of the Soul* (Nashville: Thomas Nelson, 2003).

8. Matthew 7:16

9. For more on assigning work to change attitudes, and other parenting tools to change your child's attitude, not just behavior, see Steve Sherbondy, *Changing Your Child's Heart* (Wheaton: Tyndale, 1998).

10. Winston Churchill, ThinkExist.com, Copyright ThinkExist 1999–2004, http://en.thinkexist.com/quotation/never-never-never-never_give_up/15825.html.

Chapter 4: Don't Tell Me *That* Old, Old Story

1. Liz Curtis Higgs, "Life with Liz: Guess What Junior Said Today," *Today's Christian Woman*, January/February 1999, 50.

2. Franklin Graham, *Rebel with a Cause* (Nashville: Thomas Nelson, 1995), 119–20. Reprinted with permission, all rights reserved.

3. Ibid., 122–23.

4. Tevye, *Fiddler on the Roof*, The Internet Movie Database, Copyright 1990, 2005, http://www.imdb.com/title/tt0067093/quotes.

5. Esther 4:14

6. 2 Timothy 1:5

7. Luke 15:11–32

8. Genesis 4:1–16

9. Genesis 12:1–9; 13:1–13; 18:16–19:38

10. 1 Samuel 2:12; the full story is in 1 Samuel 2:12–4:11.

11. Acts 13:22; the story of Absalom's rebellion is found in 2 Samuel 15–18.

12. Ephesians 1:11

13. 2 Corinthians 6:20

14. Gary Thomas, *Sacred Pathways* (Grand Rapids: Zondervan, 1996).

15. Ibid., 28.

16. From Proverbs 22:1, my translation

17. From 1 Corinthians 15:33, my translation

18. Matthew 6:22

19. From 2 Timothy 2:22, my translation

20. From Ephesians 4:29, my translation

21. Proverbs 29:11

22. Matthew 11:28

Chapter 5: Are You Sure You Want to Die on That Hill?

1. Garrison Keillor, Copyright 2004 BrainyMedia.com, Xplore, Inc., http://www.brainyquote.com/quotes/authors/g/garrison_keillor.html.

2. Jeff VanVonderen, *Families Where Grace Is in Place* (Minneapolis: Bethany, 1992).

3. 2 Thessalonians 3:10

Chapter 6: Be All That You Can Be

1. Paula Poundstone, Copyright 2004 BrainyMedia.com, Xplore, Inc., http://www.brainyquote.com/quotes/authors/p/paula_poundstone.html.

2. U.S. Census Bureau. March Current Population Survey. Income Statistics Branch/HHES Division. U.S. Department of Commerce: Washington, DC. Table F-18 (www.census.gov/hhes/income/histinc/f018.html).

3. Ron Blue, *Master Your Money* (Nashville: Thomas Nelson, 1986).

4. Ron Blue and Judy Blue, *Raising Money-Smart Kids* (Nashville: Thomas Nelson, 1992).

5. Gregg Easterbrook, *The Progress Paradox: How Life Gets Better While People Feel Worse* (New York: Random House, 2003).

6. Matthew 6:19–20

7. Author unknown. An extensive search was made to determine the original author. It has been attributed to numerous individuals or contributors to publications, web sites, and the like, but its origins are uncertain.

8. Paul D. Tieger and Barbara Barron Tieger, *Do What You Are* (Boston: Little, Brown, 2001).

Chapter 7: Umbilical Cords, Apron Strings, and Phone Lines

1. Jone Johnson Lewis, "Women's History: Erma Bombeck Quotes," About.com, http://womenshistory.about.com/cs/quotes/a/qu_erma_bombeck_2.htm (accessed May 2005).

2. W. Bruce Cameron, *8 Simple Rules for Dating My Teenage Daughter and other Tips from a Beleaguered Father, Not That Any of Them Work* (New York: Workman, 2001), 312–15. Used by permission, all rights reserved.

3. William Bridges, *Transitions: Making Sense of Life's Changes* (New York: Perseus Books Group, 1980), 34.

4. From Matthew 16:26

Chapter 8: You *Can* Take It with You

1. Dennis Miller, ThinkExist.com, Copyright ThinkExist 1999–2004, http://en.thinkexist.com/quotes/dennis_miller/3.html.

Russ Robinson is coauthor of three books, including *Walking the Small Group Tightrope*. He is now an attorney in Chicago—the "day job" that permits his frequent speaking and consulting for churches and other organizations. Russ has been both an elder and the Director of Ministries and Small Groups at Willow Creek Community Church, where he continues to attend. He also served as senior pastor of Meadowbrook Church in North Haledon, New Jersey.

Married since 1977, Russ and Lynn are parents to three children. Phil is a college student loving life in his new home away from home. Mark and Tim are navigating their way through high school, both of them aspiring jazz musicians when girls, jobs, and cars permit it. Lynn survives the male-dominated household by her quilting and other art crafts . . . and the protection of her dog, Cooper.